P9-CPW-579

Cases in Finance

Jim DeMello
Western Michigan University

**McGraw-Hill
Irwin**

Boston   Burr Ridge, IL   Dubuque, IA   Madison, WI   New York   San Francisco   St. Louis
Bangkok   Bogotá   Caracas   Kuala Lumpur   Lisbon   London   Madrid   Mexico City
Milan   Montreal   New Delhi   Santiago   Seoul   Singapore   Sydney   Taipei   Toronto

McGraw-Hill Higher Education

*A Division of The **McGraw·Hill** Companies*

CASES IN FINANCE
Jim DeMello

Published by McGraw-Hill/Irwin, an imprint of The McGraw-Hill Companies, Inc., 1221 Avenue of the Americas, New York, NY 10020. Copyright © 2003 by The McGraw-Hill Companies, Inc. All rights reserved.
No part of this publication may be reproduced or distributed in any form or by any means, or stored in a database or retrieval system, without the prior written consent of The McGraw-Hill Companies, Inc., including, but not limited to, in any network or other electronic storage or transmission, or broadcast for distance learning.

2 3 4 5 6 7 8 9 0 FGR/FGR 0 9 8 7 6 5 4 3

ISBN 0-07-253632-2

www.mhhe.com

The McGraw-Hill/Irwin Series in Finance, Insurance and Real Estate

Stephen A. Ross
Franco Modigliani Professor of Finance and Economics
Sloan School of Management
Massachusetts Institute of Technology
Consulting Editor

FINANCIAL MANAGEMENT

Benninga and Sarig
Corporate Finance: A Valuation Approach

Block and Hirt
Foundations of Financial Management
Tenth Edition

Brealey and Myers
Principles of Corporate Finance
Seventh Edition

Brealey, Myers and Marcus
Fundamentals of Corporate Finance
Third Edition

Brooks
FinGame Online 3.0

Bruner
Case Studies in Finance: Managing for
Corporate Value Creation
Fourth Edition

Chew
The New Corporate Finance: Where
Theory Meets Practice
Third Edition

DeMello
Cases in Finance

Grinblatt and Titman
Financial Markets and Corporate Strategy
Second Edition

Helfert
Techniques of Financial Analysis: A Guide
to Value Creation
Eleventh Edition

Higgins
Analysis for Financial Management
Seventh Edition

Kester, Fruhan, Piper and Ruback
Case Problems in Finance
Eleventh Edition

Nunnally and Plath
Cases in Finance
Second Edition

Ross, Westerfield and Jaffe
Corporate Finance
Sixth Edition

Ross, Westerfield and Jordan
Essentials of Corporate Finance
Third Edition

Ross, Westerfield and Jordan
Fundamentals of Corporate Finance
Sixth Edition

Smith
The Modern Theory of Corporate Finance
Second Edition

White
Financial Analysis with an Electronic
Calculator
Fourth Edition

INVESTMENTS

Bodie, Kane and Marcus
Essentials of Investments
Fourth Edition

Bodie, Kane and Marcus
Investments
Fifth Edition

Cohen, Zinbarg and Zeikel
Investment Analysis and Portfolio
Management
Fifth Edition

Corrado and Jordan
Fundamentals of Investments: Valuation
and Management
Second Edition

Farrell
Portfolio Management: Theory and
Applications
Second Edition

Hirt and Block
Fundamentals of Investment Management
Seventh Edition

FINANCIAL INSTITUTIONS AND MARKETS

Cornett and Saunders
Fundamentals of Financial Institutions
Management

Rose
Commercial Bank Management
Sixth Edition

Rose
Money and Capital Markets: Financial
Institutions and Instruments in a Global
Marketplace
Eighth Edition

Santomero and Babbel
Financial Markets, Instruments, and
Institutions
Second Edition

Saunders and Cornett
Financial Institutions Management: A Risk
Management Approach
Fourth Edition

Saunders and Cornett
Financial Markets and Institutions: A
Modern Perspective

INTERNATIONAL FINANCE

Beim and Calomiris
Emerging Financial Markets

Eun and Resnick
International Financial Management
Second Edition

Levich
International Financial Markets: Prices and
Policies
Second Edition

REAL ESTATE

Brueggeman and Fisher
Real Estate Finance and Investments
Eleventh Edition

Corgel, Ling and Smith
Real Estate Perspectives: An Introduction
to Real Estate
Fourth Edition

FINANCIAL PLANNING AND INSURANCE

Allen, Melone, Rosenbloom and Mahoney
Pension Planning: Pension, Profit-Sharing,
and Other Deferred Compensation Plans
Ninth Edition

Crawford
Life and Health Insurance Law
Eighth Edition (LOMA)

Harrington and Niehaus
Risk Management and Insurance

Hirsch
Casualty Claim Practice
Sixth Edition

Kapoor, Dlabay and Hughes
Personal Finance
Sixth Edition

Skipper
International Risk and Insurance: An
Environmental-Managerial Approach

Williams, Smith and Young
Risk Management and Insurance
Eighth Edition

Introduction

Cases in Finance has been developed to enhance the key concepts of an introductory corporate finance text. The cases in this book present these concepts within a realistic setting, and are accompanied by questions and problems that assist students in applying these concepts to business decision making.

These cases are hypothetical: they take place within a believable business setting, yet the numbers always work out neatly to allow students to focus on one issue at a time. Once the calculations are done, students move beyond them via the questions and problems, which introduce a strong element of critical thinking and analysis.

Cases in Finance is supported by Teaching Notes which include solutions to each case and how to solve the questions in Excel, and PowerPoint slides that outline the cases and solutions for instructors interested in presenting and discussing the cases in class.

Table of Contents

1

Cash Flow Analysis

Signal Cable Company

When Jay Smith took the job of Assistant to the President, two years ago, things were going rather well at the Signal Cable Company. The company was on an expansionary path and had branched off into the fiber optics business. The prospects looked good and the economy was strong. The threat of competition was not too severe. Due to the expectation of increased demand for fiber optic communications, the company had established two additional manufacturing facilities, and significantly increased its inventory.

Signal Cable had quite a run up in profits over the past few years. However, when the accounting statements were prepared for the current year, the results showed a lower profitability. More importantly, there was a severe drop in the cash balance of the company and the stock price had recently fallen from $7 to $5.50 per share.

Jay knew that the shareholders would be very concerned and possibly irate. He was also sure that his boss, Joe Mathis would have to come up with some feasible answers and suggestions as to how the liquidity problems could be alleviated. This concern was primarily important since the firm had been expecting to raise some short-term capital in the immediate future. Jay's expectations were fulfilled when Joe called him up and asked him to prepare a report explaining the financial condition of the firm. Table I and II present the Income statement and Balance Sheet for the recent two years.

Table 1

Income Statement

	2001	2000
Net Sales	2,050,000	1,678,894
Cost of Goods sold	1,537,500	1,343,115
Depreciation	79,000	51,000
Selling & Administrative Expenses	40,000	32,945
Earnings Before Interest and Taxes	393,500	251,833.8
Interest Paid	155,000	44,000
Taxable Income	238,500	207,833.8
Taxes (40%)	95,400	83,133.52
Net Income	143,100	124,700.3
Dividends	42,930	37,410.08
Addition to Retained Earnings	100,170	87,290.2

Table 2

Balance Sheet

	2001	2000
ASSETS		
Cash	5,000	40,000
Accounts Receivable	540,000	200,000
Inventories	1,300,450	650,000
Total Current Assets	1,845,450	890,000
NWC	950,450	535,000
Gross Fixed Assets	1,300,000	510,000
Accumulated Depreciation	232,000	153,000
Net Fixed Assets	1,068,000	357,000
Total Assets	2,913,450	1,247,000
LIABILITIES & EQUITY		
Accounts Payable	145,000	55,000
Notes Payable	750,000	300,000
Total Current Liabilities	895,000	355,000
Long-term Debt	1,226,280	200,000
Common-stock and Paid in Surplus (200,000 shares outstanding)	600,000	600,000
Retained Earnings	192,170	92,000
Total	2,913,450	1,247,000

Questions:

1. Why has the stock price fallen in spite of the fact that the Net Income has increased?

2. How liquid would you say that this company is? Calculate the absolute liquidity of the firm. How does it compare with the previous year's liquidity position?

3. How does the market value of the stock compare with its book value? Is the book value accurately reflecting the true condition of the company?

4. The board of directors are not clear as to why the cash balance has dropped so much in spite of the increase in sales and the reduction in cost of goods sold. What should Jay tell them?

5. Measure the free cash flow of the firm. What does it indicate?

6. Calculate the net working capital of the company for each of the two years. What can you conclude about the firm's net working capital?

2

Financial Ratio Analysis

Bigger Isn't Always Better!

Andre Pires opened his automobile parts store, Quickfix Auto Parts, in 1997, in a mid-sized city located in the mid-western region of the United States. Having worked for an automobile dealership, first as a technician, and later as the parts department manager, for over 15 years, Andre had learned the many nuances of the fiercely competitive automobile servicing business. He had developed many contacts with dealers and service technicians, which came in real handy when establishing his own retail store. Business had picked up significantly well over the years, and as a result, Andre had more than doubled his store size by the third year of operations. The industry and local forecasts for the next few years were very good and Andre was confident that his sales would keep growing at or above the recent levels.

However, Andre had used up most of his available funds in expanding the business and was well aware that future growth would have to be funded with external funds. What was worrying Andre was the fact that over the past two years, the store's net income figures had been negative, and his cash flow situation had gotten pretty weak (See Tables 1 and 2). He figured that he had better take a good look at his firm's financial situation and try to improve it, if possible, before his suppliers found out. He knew fully well that being shut out by suppliers would be disastrous!

Andre's knowledge of finance and accounting, not unlike many small businessmen, was very limited. He had often entertained the thought of taking some financial management courses, but could never find the time. One day, at his weekly bridge session, he happened to mention his problem to Tom Andrews, his long time friend and bridge partner. Tom had often given him good advice in the past and Andre was desperate for a solution. "I'm no finance expert, Andre," said Tom, "but you might want to contact the finance department at our local university's business school and see if you can hire an MBA student as an intern. These students can often be very insightful, you know."

That's exactly what Andre did. Within a week he was able to recruit Juan Plexo, a second semester MBA student, who had an undergraduate degree in Accountancy and was interested in concentrating in Finance. When Juan started his internship, Andre explained exactly what his concerns were. "I'm going to have to raise funds for future growth, and given my recent profit situation, the prospects look pretty bleak. I can't seem to put my finger on the exact cause. The commercial loan committee is going to want some pretty convincing arguments as to why they should grant me the loan. I had better put some concrete remedial measures in place. I was hoping that you can help sort things out, Juan," said Andre. " I think I may have bitten off more than I can currently chew."

Table 1

Quickfix Autoparts Balance Sheet					
ASSETS	**1997**	**1998**	**1999**	**2000**	**2001**
Cash and marketable securities	$155,000	$309,099	$75,948	$28,826	$18,425
Accounts receivable	10,000	12,000	20,000	77,653	90,078
Inventory	250,000	270,000	500,000	520,000	560,000
Current assets	$415,000	$591,099	$595,948	$626,480	$668,503
Land, buildings, plant, and equipment	$250,000	$250,000	$500,000	$500,000	$500,000
Accumulated depreciation	(25,000)	(50,000)	(100,000)	(150,000)	(200,000)
Net fixed assets	$225,000	$200,000	$400,000	$350,000	$300,000
Total assets	$640,000	$791,099	$995,948	$976,480	$968,503
LIABILITIES AND EQUITIES					
Short-term bank loans	$50,000	$145,000	$140,000	$148,000	$148,000
Accounts payable	10,000	10,506	19,998	15,995	16,795
Accruals	5,000	5,100	7,331	9,301	11,626
Current liabilities	$165,000	$160,606	$167,329	$173,296	$176,421
Long-term bank loans	$63,366	$98,000	$196,000	$190,000	$183,000
Mortgage	175,000	173,000	271,000	268,000	264,000
Long-term debt	$238,366	$271,000	$467,000	$458,000	$447,000
Total liabilities	$303,366	$431,606	$634,329	$631,296	$623,421
Common stock (100,000 shares)	$320,000	$320,000	$320,000	$320,000	$320,000
Retained earnings	16,634	39,493	41,619	25,184	25,082
Total equity	$336,634	$359,493	$361,619	$345,184	$345,082
Total liabilities and equity	$640,000	$791,099	$995,948	$976,480	$968,503

Table 2

Quickfix Autoparts *Income Statement*					
	1997	**1998**	**1999**	**2000**	**2001**
Net sales	$600,000	$655,000	$780,000	$873,600	$1,013,376
Cost of goods sold	480,000	537,100	655,200	742,560	861,370
Gross profit	$120,000	$117,900	$124,800	$131,040	$152,006
Admin and selling exp	$30,000	$15,345	$16,881	$43,680	$40,535
Depreciation	25,000	25,000	50,000	50,000	50,000
Miscellaneous expenses	2,027	3,557	5,725	17,472	15,201
Total operating exp	$57,027	$43,902	$72,606	$111,152	$105,736
EBIT	$62,973	$73,998	$52,194	$19,888	$46,271
Interest on ST loans	$15,000	$15,950	$14,000	$13,320	$13,320
Interest on LT loans	8,000	7,840	15,680	15,200	14,640
Interest on mortgage	12,250	12,110	18,970	18,760	18,480
Total interest	$35,250	$35,900	$48,650	$47,280	$46,440
Before-tax earnings	$27,723	$38,098	$3,544	($27,392)	($169)
Taxes	11,089	15,239	1,418	(10,957)	(68)
Net income	$16,634	$22,859	$2,126	($16,435)	($102)
Dividends on stock	0	0	0	0	0
Additions to retained earnings	$16,634	$22,859	$2,126	($16,435)	($102)
EPS (100,000 shares)	$0.17	$0.23	$0.02	($0.16)	($0.00)

Questions:

1. How does Quickfix's average compound growth rate in sales compare with its earnings growth rate over the past five years?

2. Which statements should Juan refer to and which one's should he construct so as to develop a fair assessment of the firm's financial condition? Explain why?

3. What calculations should Juan do in order to get a good grasp of what is going on with Quickfix's performance?

4. Juan knows that he should compare Quickfix's condition with an appropriate benchmark. How should he go about obtaining the necessary comparison data?

5. Besides comparison with the benchmark what other types of analyses could Juan perform to comprehensively analyze the firm's condition? Perform the suggested analyses and comment on your findings.

6. Comment on Quickfix's liquidity, asset utilization, long-term solvency, and profitability ratios. What arguments would have to be made to convince the bank that they should grant Quickfix the loan?

7. If you were the commercial loan officer and were approached by Andre for a short-term loan of $25,000, what would your decision be? Why?

8. What recommendations should Juan make for improvement, if any?

9. What kinds of problems do you think Juan would have to cope with when doing a comprehensive financial statement analysis of Quickfix Auto Parts? What are the limitations of financial statement analysis in general?

3

DuPont Analysis

Playing the Numbers Game!

"Numbers! I need to see numbers!" exclaimed Andrew in response to comments made by the assistant vice-president of Finance, Jack Brown. Andrew Sullivan, the President and Chief Executive Officer of Plastichem Inc. had been instrumental in significantly increasing the company's size during his first five years in office. He spearheaded some successful marketing campaigns and revamped the production facilities by adopting the latest technology in injection molding. He also implemented various cost-cutting measures and introduced performance plans to boost efficiency. Foremen and supervisors were offered stock option incentives, and bonuses were tied to earnings per share (EPS) growth.

Plastichem Inc., a medium-sized plastic molding company was founded in 1990 and was located in Midland, Michigan. The company supplied molded plastic products to various processing industries as well as end-users. It enjoyed a fairly diversified base of customers ranging from automobile and home products manufacturers to the federal government. After an initial period of sluggish growth, the firm's revenues and profits had almost quadrupled. Most of the increase had been achieved under the leadership of Andrew Sullivan. The plastics business offered potential for high profit margins and as a result it attracted many competitors. Despite the fierce competition, Plastichem's stock which traded in the Over-the-Counter market, had tripled in value over the past five years making the shareholders very happy.

Recently, however, the stock price had dipped sharply, raising concerns among security analysts. Jack Brown, the assistant VP of Finance, brought this matter to Andrew's attention informing him that the analysts had given their closest rival, DCM Molding, a "Strong Buy" rating while downgrading Plastichem's rating to a "Hold." This recent development had outraged shareholders and the Personal Relations department had been overwhelmed with calls from anxious owners wanting to know what was going on.

Andrew, a motivated leader, was not about to give up easily, however. His track record of turning companies around was very good. He knew that if he could identify the main problem areas, he would be able to make some strategic moves to alleviate the problems. He, therefore, demanded that he be given a detailed report of the firm's financial condition in comparison to that of DCM Molding. Andrew had learned over the years that in order to be successful it is very important to "play the numbers game."

Questions:

1. Jack Brown realizes that the first thing he must do is compare the liquidity, leverage, activity, and profitability ratios of the two companies. Using the income statement and balance sheet data shown in Tables 1 – 4, prepare a detailed comparison report indicating the strengths and weaknesses of each company.

2. Prepare and analyze the statement of cash flows for each firm. What additional information does such an analysis provide?

2.   Jay Singh, a recently hired intern has suggested to Jack that he should include an analysis of common size statements in the report. Is Jay right? Of what use is such an analysis? Please prepare such an analysis and explain your answer.

3.   Jay has also recommended that a DuPont analysis be done. How can such an analysis be performed and what information does it indicate about the relative performance of the two companies?

4.   What are some of the limitations regarding the various analyses that have been suggested above? What additional data would Jay and Jack need to improve their findings? Are there any other calculations and comparisons that would be helpful?

5.   After collecting, compiling, and analyzing the data, what conclusions and recommendations would Jack be justified in making in his report to Andrew?

6.   In your opinion, how acute is the problem facing Plastichem, Inc.? What strategic moves do you think Andrew could make to alleviate the problems?

7.   How accurate are the analysts in their recommendations of the two firms?

Table 1

Plastichem Incorporated Annual Balance Sheets (Values in millions)				
	2001	2000	1999	1998
ASSETS				
Current Assets				
Cash and marketable securities	3.2	4.8	5.0	0.6
Accounts receivable	46.1	59.6	50.1	20.9
Inventory	27.4	24.1	25.3	12.8
Other Current assets	4.1	7.6	6.9	0.4
Total Current Assets	80.8	96.1	87.3	34.7
Non-Current Assets				
Property, Plant & Equipment, Gross	94.2	98.7	87.9	47.7
Accumulated depreciation & Depletion	38.3	31.4	27.7	19.3
Property, Plant & Equipment, Net	55.9	67.3	60.2	28.4
Intangibles	121.4	172.2	182.0	32.8
Other Non-Current Assets	7.7	8.3	10.5	3.5
Total Non-Current Assets	185.0	247.8	252.7	64.7
Total Assets	**265.8**	**343.9**	**340.0**	**99.4**
LIABILITIES AND EQUITIES				
Current Liabilities				
Accounts payable	20.5	23.8	20.5	9.7
Short Term Debt	6.6	5.6	3.5	3.9
Other Current Liabilities	35.0	33.7	35.7	12.9
Total Current Liabilities	62.1	63.1	59.7	26.5
Non-Current Liabilities				
Long-term debt	215.2	221.3	222.3	30.7
Deferred Income Taxes	0.0	0.0	0.0	0.0
Other Non-Current Liabilities	3.0	2.9	0	0
Minority Interest	0.0	0.0	0.0	0.0
Total Non-Current Liabilities	218.2	224.2	222.3	30.7
Total Liabilities	**280.3**	**287.3**	**282.0**	**57.2**
Shareholder's Equity				
Preferred Stock Equity	0.0	0.0	0.0	0.0
Common Stock Equity	-14.5	56.6	58.0	42.2
Total equity	-14.5	56.6	58.0	42.2
Total liabilities and Stock Equity	**265.8**	**343.9**	**340.0**	**99.4**
Total Common Shares outstanding	7.7 Mil	7.2 Mil	7.6 Mil	6.6 Mil
Preferred Shares	0.0	0.0	0.0	0.0
Treasury Shares	0.0	0.0	0.0	0.0

Table 2

DCM Molding Annual Balance Sheets (Values in millions)				
	2001	2000	1999	1998
ASSETS				
Current Assets				
Cash and marketable securities	0.3	1.1	0.3	2.9
Accounts receivable	17.9	16.1	13.0	7.0
Inventory	12.9	11.7	9.4	3.9
Other Current assets	1.7	1.3	1.4	1.7
Total Current Assets	32.8	30.2	24.1	15.5
Non-Current Assets				
Property, Plant & Equipment, Gross	42.6	36.9	27.8	20.3
Accumulated depreciation & Depletion	15.5	11.1	7.1	3.9
Property, Plant & Equipment, Net	27.1	25.8	20.7	16.4
Intangibles	30.0	31.1	18.2	1.9
Other Non-Current Assets	0.2	0.6	1.0	2.2
Total Non-Current Assets	57.3	57.5	39.9	20.5
Total Assets	**90.1**	**87.7**	**64.0**	**36.0**
LIABILITIES AND EQUITIES				
Current Liabilities				
Accounts payable	6.9	7.1	5.3	2.0
Short Term Debt	6.7	5.8	2.7	2.7
Other current Liabilities	6.5	7.1	5.3	2.7
Total Current liabilities	20.1	19.9	13.2	7.4
Non-Current liabilities				
Long-term debt	25.8	28.0	18.7	5.4
Deferred Income Taxes	0.1	0.5	0.0	1.4
Other Non-Current Liabilities	3.0	3.9	3.9	0.8
Minority Interest	0.0	0.0	0.0	0.0
Total Non-Current Liabilities	28.9	32.4	22.6	7.6
Total Liabilities	**49.0**	**52.3**	**35.8**	**15.0**
Shareholder's Equity				
Preferred Stock Equity	0.0	0.0	0.0	0.0
Common Stock Equity	41.1	35.4	28.1	21.0
Total equity	41.1	35.4	28.1	21.0
Total liabilities and Stock Equity	**90.1**	**87.7**	**64.0**	**36.0**
Total Common Shares outstanding	4.3 mil	4.3 mil	4.3 mil	4.1 mil
Preferred Shares	0.0	0.0	0.0	0.0
Treasury Shares	0.0	0.0	0.0	0.0

Table 3

Plastichem Incorporated Annual Income Statements (Value in Millions)				
	2001	2000	1999	1998
Sales	297.0	294.0	252.4	129.3
Cost of Sales	222.2	184.5	160.0	84.1
Gross Operating profit	74.8	109.5	92.4	45.2
Selling, General & Admin. Expenses	39.4	54.5	47.1	26.8
EBITDA	35.4	55.0	45.3	18.4
Depreciation & Amortization	18.3	16.2	14.7	5.7
EBIT	17.1	38.8	30.6	12.7
Other Income, Net	-0.5	0.6	0.3	0.1
Total Income Avail for Interest Exp.	-49.2	24.4	30.9	12.8
Interest Expense	22.4	20.3	15.6	5.2
Minority Interest	0.0	0.0	0.0	0.0
Pre-Tax Income	-71.6	4.1	15.3	7.6
Income Taxes	0.1	2.1	6.6	0.3
Special Income/Charges	-65.8	-15.0	0.0	0.0
Net Income from Cont.Operations	-71.5	2.0	8.8	7.3
Net Income from Discont. Opers.	0.0	0.0	0.0	0.0
Net Income from Total Operations	-71.5	2.0	8.8	7.3
Normalized Income	-5.7	17.0	8.8	7.3
Extraordinary Income	0.0	0.0	0.0	0.0
Income from Cum. Eff.of Acct. Chg.	0.0	0.0	0.0	0.0
Income from Tax Loss Carryforward	0.0	0.0	0.0	0.0
Other Gains	0.0	0.0	-5.1	0.0
Total Net Income	**-71.5**	**2.0**	**3.7**	**7.3**

Table 4

DCM Molding Annual Income Statements (Value in Millions)				
	2001	2000	1999	1998
Sales	123.6	106.7	85.7	43.2
Cost of Sales	82.6	69.2	55.5	27.2
Gross Operating profit	41.0	37.5	30.2	16.0
Selling, General & Admin. Expenses	21.3	19.9	16.8	9.6
EBITDA	19.7	17.6	13.4	6.4
Depreciation & Amortization	5.7	4.7	3.7	2.1
EBIT	14.0	12.9	9.7	4.3
Other Income, Net	0.0	0.0	-0.1	-0.1
Total Income Avail for Interest Exp.	14.0	12.9	9.6	4.2
Interest Expense	3.0	2.3	1.8	0.5
Minority Interest	0.0	0.0	0.0	0.0
Pre-Tax Income	11.0	10.6	7.8	3.7
Income Taxes	3.7	4.0	3.2	1.5
Special Income/Charges	0.0	0.0	0.0	0.0
Net Income from Cont.Operations	7.3	6.6	4.6	2.3
Net Income from Discont. Opers.	0.0	0.0	0.3	0.0
Net Income from Total Operations	7.3	6.6	4.9	2.3
Normalized Income	7.3	6.6	4.6	2.3
Extraordinary Income	0.0	0.0	0.0	0.0
Income from Cum. Eff of Acct. Chg.	0.0	0.0	0.0	0.0
Income from Tax Loss Carryforward	0.0	0.0	0.0	0.0
Other Gains	0.0	0.0	0.0	0.0
Total Net Income	**7.3**	**6.6**	**4.9**	**2.3**

4

Financial Forecasting

Growing Pains

"We are growing too fast," said Lynn. "I know I shouldn't complain, but we better have the capacity to fill the orders or we'll be hurting ourselves." Bonnie and Lynn Rogers started their oatmeal snacks company in 1995, upon the suggestions of their close friends who simply loved the way their oatmeal tasted. Lynn, a former college gymnastics coach insists that he never "intended to start a business," but the thought of being able to support his college team played a significant role in motivating him to go for it.

After considerable help from local retailers and a sponsorship by a major bread company their firm, Oats Unlimited, was established in 1995 and reached sales of over $4 million by 2001. Given the current trend of eating healthy snacks and keeping fit, Lynn was confident that sales would increase significantly over the next few years. The industry growth forecast had been estimated at 30% per year and Lynn was confident that his firm would be able to at least achieve if not beat that rate of sales growth.

"We must plan for the future," said Bonnie. "I think we've been playing it by ear for too long." Lynn immediately called for the treasurer, John Alves. "John, I need to know how much additional funding we are going to need for the next year," said Lynn. "The growth rate of revenues should be between 25% and 40%. I would really appreciate if you can have the forecast on my desk by early next week."

John knew that his fishing plans for the weekend had better be put aside coz it was going to be a long and busy weekend for him. He immediately asked the accounting department to give him the last three years' financial statements (see Table 1 and 2) and got right to work!

Questions:

1.   Since this is the first time John and Lynn will be conducting a financial forecast for Oats Unlimited, how do you think they should proceed? Which approaches or models can they use? What are the assumptions necessary for utilizing each model?

2.   If Oats Unlimited is operating its fixed assets at full capacity, what growth rate can it support without the need for any additional external financing?

3.   Oats Unlimited has a flexible credit line with the Midland Bank. If Lynn decides to keep the debt-equity ratio constant, what rate of growth in revenues can the firm support? What assumptions are necessary when calculating this rate of growth? Are these assumptions realistic in the case of Oats Unlimited? Please explain.

4.   Initially John assumes that the firm is operating at full capacity. How much additional financing will it need to support revenue growth rates ranging from 25% to 40% per year?

5.   After conducting an interview with the production manager, John realizes that Oats Unlimited is operating its plant at 90% capacity, how much additional financing will it need to support growth rates ranging from 25% to 40%?

6.   What are some actions that Lynn can take in order to alleviate some of the need for external financing? Analyze the feasibility and implications of each suggested action.

7.   How critical is the financial condition of Oats Unlimited? Is Bonnie justified in being concerned about the need for financial planning? Explain why.

8.   Given that Lynn prefers not to deviate from the firm's 2001 debt-equity ratio, what will the firm's pro-forma income statement and balance sheet look like under the scenario of 40% growth in revenue for 2002 (ignore feedback effects)

Table 1

Oats Unlimited			
Income Statement			
For the Year Ended Dec. 31st 2001			
	2001	*2000*	*1999*
Sales	4,700,000	3,760,000	3,000,000
Cost of Goods Sold	3,877,500	3,045,600	2,400,000
Gross Profit	*822,500*	*714,400*	*600,000*
Selling and G&A Expenses	275,000	250,000	215,000
Fixed Expenses	90,000	90,000	90,000
Depreciation Expense	25,000	25,000	25,000
Earnings Before Interest and Taxes	*432,500*	*349,400*	*270,000*
Interest Expense	66,000	66,000	66,000
Earnings Before Taxes	*366,500*	*283,400*	*204,000*
Taxes @ 40%	146600	113360	81600
Net Income	*219,900*	*170,040*	*122,400*
Retained Earnings	131940	102024	73440

Table 2

Oats Unlimited Balance Sheet For the Year Ended Dec. 31st 2001			
Assets	**2001**	*2000*	*1999*
Cash and Cash Equivalents	60,000	50,000	48,000
Accounts Receivable	250,416	175,000	150,000
Inventory	511,500	390,000	335,000
Total Current Assets	*821,916*	*615,000*	*533,000*
Plant & Equipment	560,000	560,000	560,000
Accumulated Depreciation	175,000	150,000	125,000
Net Plant & Equipment	385,000	410,000	435,000
Total Assets	**1,206,916**	**1,025,000**	**968,000**
Liabilities and Owner's Equity			
Accounts Payable	135,000	151,352	128,000
Notes Payable	275,000	275,000	250,000
Other Current Liabilities	43,952	50,000	46,000
Total Current Liabilities	*453,952*	*476,352*	*424,000*
Long-term Debt	275,000	250,000	300,000
Total Liabilities	*728,952*	*726,352*	*724,000*
Owner's Capital	155,560	155,560	155,560
Retained Earnings	322,404	190,464	88,440
Total Liabilities and Owner's Equity	**1,206,916**	**1,025,000**	**968,000**

5

Time Value of Money

Lottery Winnings – Looks Can Be Deceptive!

State-sponsored lotteries are extremely popular and highly successful methods by which state governments in many countries raise much needed funds for financing public expenses, especially education. In Michigan alone, during the year 2000, Michigan Lottery reported annual sales of $1.69 billion in fiscal 2000, and generated $618.5 million in net revenue for the state School Aid Fund, supporting public education (K-12) programs throughout the state. Retailers received annual commissions of $120.3 million, while Michigan Lottery players collected prizes worth $920.8 million. Table I presents sales and funding figures accounted for by the Michigan Lottery since its inception in 1972. The numbers are quite impressive.

Table 1

Totals: 1972 Start-up through FY 2000*

Total Lottery Ticket Sales	**$25.12 billion**
Net Revenue to Aid Education	**$9.83 billion**
Retailer Commissions	**$1.68 billion**
Prizes to Players	**$12.86 billion**

*http://www.Michigan.gov/lottery

The Big Game is a multi-state lottery game with BIG Jackpots. Seven states participate in The Big Game: Georgia, Illinois, Maryland, Massachusetts, Michigan, New Jersey and Virginia. By teaming up together, the member lotteries are able to offer players jackpots that start at $5 million. The jackpots grow until someone wins. Jackpots can grow as high as $200 million or more. In fact, The Big Game holds the record for the largest lottery jackpot ever in the United States: $363 million! This jackpot rolled 18 times since last being hit! Two winning tickets -- one sold in Michigan, and one sold in Illinois -- matched all six numbers in this Big Game drawing, each worth an annuitized value of $181.5 million. The winners were Larry and Nancy Ross of Shelby Township, Michigan, and Joe and Sue Kainz of Lake County, Illinois.

The Michigan Lottery can pay Big Game jackpot winnings in one of two ways: as an annuity or in one lump-sum/cash-option payment for the present cash value of the jackpot share. When a winner selects annuity payments, the jackpot is paid out in equal installments over 26 years. When a winner selects the cash option, the Lottery pays the winner the present cash value of the announced jackpot in one lump-sum payment, which is typically about 50% of the published value. In effect, the Lottery takes all of the money that would have been invested to fund the 26-year annuity and turns it all over to the winner, retaining absolutely none of the prize. Regardless of which option the winner selects, the Michigan Lottery is required by law to withhold estimated income taxes for federal (28 percent) and state (4.2 percent), on any prize over $5,000. These amounts are estimates only, and the winner is required to satisfy any further tax liability for the year in which the prize award is claimed.

Questions:

1. If you were one of the winners, which option would you select? Why?

2. If you decide to select the annuity option, how much money would you receive each year after taxes?

3. Is the State of Michigan justified in advertising the prize amount as $363 million? Explain.

4. If the only option available were an annuity payment plan, what could Larry do to maximize the value of his winnings assuming that the risk-free rate of interest is 5%.

5. Why do most winners select the cash option plan when given a choice?

6. If Michigan Lottery would like to give the annuity option an equal chance of being selected, how would it have to structure its payments?

6

Retirement Planning

Saving for Retirement? Better Late Than Never!

"Boy, this is all so confusing," said John as he stared at the papers on his desk. If only I had taken the advice of my finance instructor, I would not be in such a predicament today." John Andrews, aged 27, graduated five years ago with a degree in business administration and is currently employed as a middle-level manager for a fairly successful grocery chain. His current annual salary of $60,000 has increased at an average rate of 5 percent per year and is projected to increase at least at that rate for the foreseeable future. The firm has had a voluntary retirement savings program in place, whereby, employees can contribute up to 11% of their gross annual salary (up to a maximum of $11,000 per year) and the company will match every dollar that the employee contributes. Unfortunately, like many other young people who start out in their first 'real' job, John has not yet taken advantage of the retirement savings program. He opted instead to buy a fancy car, rent an expensive apartment, and consume most of his income.

However, with wedding plans on the horizon, John has finally come to the realization that he had better start putting away some money for the future. His fiancé, Mary, of course, had a lot to do with giving him this reality check. Mary reminded John that besides retirement, there were various other large expenses that would be forthcoming and that it would be wise for him to design a comprehensive savings plan, keeping in mind the various approximate costs and timelines involved.

John figures that the two largest expenses down the road would be those related to the wedding and down payment on a house. He estimates that the wedding, which will take place in twelve months, should cost about $10,000 in today's dollars. Furthermore, he plans to move into a $200,000 house (in today's terms) after 5 years, and would need 20% for a down payment. John is aware that his cost estimates are in current terms and would need to be adjusted for inflation. Moreover, he knows that an automatic payroll deduction is probably the best way to go since he is not a very disciplined investor. John is really not sure how much money he should put away each month, given the inflation effects, the differences in timelines, and the salary increases that would be forthcoming. All this number crunching seems overwhelming and the objectives seem insurmountable. If only he had started planning and saving five years ago, his financial situation would have been so much better. But, as the saying goes, "It's better late than NEVER!"

Questions:

1.   What was John's starting salary? How much could he have contributed to the voluntary savings plan in his first year of employment?

2.   Had John availed of the company's voluntary retirement plan up to the maximum, every year for the past five years, how much money would he currently have accumulated in his retirement account, assuming monthly deposits and a nominal rate of return of 6% with interest compounded monthly? How much more would his investment value be had he opted for a higher risk alternative (i.e. 100% in common stocks) which was expected to yield an average compound rate of return of 10% (A.P.R)?

3.   If John starts his retirement savings plan from January of next year by contributing the maximum allowable amount into the firm's voluntary retirement savings program, how much money will he have accumulated for retirement, assuming he retires at age 65? Assume that the rate of return on the account is 10% per year, compounded monthly.

4.   John figures he will need approximately $30,000 per year (in current dollars) during his retirement. If inflation is expected to average 4% per year and John's savings yield 10% per year, how long will his retirement savings last?

5.   How much would John have to save each month, starting from the end of the next month, in order to accumulate enough money for his wedding expenses, assuming that his investment fund is expected to yield a rate of return of 10% per year?

6.   If John starts saving immediately for the down payment on his house, how much additional money will he have to save each month? Assume an investment rate of return of 10% per year.

7.   If John wants to have a million dollars when he retires, how much should he save in equal monthly deposits from the end of the next month? Ignore the cost of the wedding and the down payment on the house. Assume his savings earn a rate of 8% per year (A.P.R.)

8.   If John saves up the million dollars by the time of his retirement at age 65, how much can he withdraw each month in equal dollar amounts, if he figures he will live up to the age of 85 years? Assume that his investment fund yields a nominal rate of return of 8% per year.

9.   After preparing a detailed budget, John estimates that the maximum he will be able to save for retirement is $250 per month, for the first five years. After that he is confident that he will be able to increase the monthly saving to $500 per month until retirement. If the account provides a nominal annual return of 8%, how much money will John be able to withdraw per month during his retirement phase?

7

Loan Amortization

Paying Off That Dream House

When June and Patrick Baker were "house hunting" five years ago, the mortgage rates were pretty high. The fixed rate on a 30-year mortgage was 8.75% while the 15-year fixed rate was at 8%. After walking through many homes, they finally reached a consensus and decided to buy a $150,000 two-story house in an up and coming suburban neighborhood in the Mid-West. To avoid prepaid mortgage insurance (PMI) the couple had to borrow from family members and come up with the 20% down payment and the additional required closing costs. Since June and Patrick had already accumulated significant credit card debt and were still paying off their college loans, they decided to opt for lower 30-year mortgage payments, despite its higher interest rate.

Currently, due to a worsening of economic conditions, mortgage rates have come down significantly and the "refinancing" frenzy is underway. June and Patrick have seen 5 year fixed rates (with no closing costs) advertised at 6% and 30-year rates at 6.75%. June and Patrick realize that refinancing is quite a hassle due to all the paper work involved but with rates being down to 30-year lows, they don't want to let this opportunity pass them by. About 2 years ago, rates were down to similar levels but they had procrastinated, and had missed the boat. This time, however the couple called their mortgage officer at the Uptown Bank and locked in the 6%, 15 year rate.

Questions:

1. What is June and Patrick's monthly mortgage payment prior to the refinancing?

2. During the first 5 years, how much has the couple paid towards the mortgage? What proportion of this was applied toward interest?

3. Had the couple opted for the 15-year mortgage for their refinancing, how much higher would their monthly payment be?

4. Under a 15-year mortgage, how much would the interest component be?

5. Since interest is tax-deductible, how much tax deduction would be lost by going to a 15-year plan?

6. If the house is currently worth $185,000, how much can they borrow?

7. Should they cash out the excess? Assume the risk-free rate is 5% and T-Bill is 3%.

8. Had they made one extra payment, equally divided over the twelve months, what would the pay off amount to?

9. Demonstrate using an amortization schedule how the Bankers can reduce the length of their mortgage down from 15 years.

10. If they refinanced, how much will they save over the years. Assume they have a tax rate of 30%, and their money can be invested at 6%.

8

Bond Analysis and Valuation

Corporate Bonds-They Are More Complex Than You Think

Jill Dougherty was hired as an investment analyst by A.M. Smith Inc. for the Cincinnati, Ohio office based on her sound academic credentials, which included an MBA from a top ranking university and a CFA designation. At the time of her recruitment she was told that one of her responsibilities would be to conduct educational seminars for current and prospective clients.

A.M. Smith Inc., a prestigious investment services firm, with branches in 30 major metropolitan areas, had achieved most of its success due to its excellent client relations and focus on client support. The firm ranked among the very best in terms of the number of successful equity underwriting deals undertaken. Recently, a large utility company had hired it as the leading investment banker, for a major corporate bond issue. Since most of its retail customers were more familiar with stock investments, John Sullivan, the branch manager at the Cincinnati office, asked Jill to prepare and present a seminar outlining the various implications of fixed income investments. "About 60% of our investors are in the 55+ age group, Jill, so we should not have much trouble convincing them of the benefits of investing in bonds" remarked John. "However, they may need clarifications regarding various terms and concepts associated with fixed income investing. Your job is to convince them of the relative safety and income potential of corporate bonds" said John.

In preparation for the seminar, Jill called up a few of her best clients and queried them regarding their awareness of the risk and return potential associated with corporate bond investments. She realized that apart from a good knowledge about the current level and stability of interest rates and inflation, most customers were not very familiar about the finer aspects of bond investing. Bond features like callability, convertibility, sinking fund provision, bond ratings, debentures, interest rate risk, etc. were not well understood by most of the clients she interviewed. Most of them seemed awfully interested in knowing more about the opportunities offered by bond investing and Jill knew that she would have a good turnout at the seminar. She decided to refer back to her Finance textbook and dig out some definitions and examples that she could use in her PowerPoint presentation. She downloaded current data for outstanding bonds of various maturities, ratings, and coupon rates (see Table 1) and started preparing her slides.

Table 1
Corporate Bond Information

Issuer	Face Value	Coupon Rate	Rating	Quoted Price	Years until maturity	Sinking Fund	Call Period
ABC Energy	$1,000	5%	AAA	$703.1	20	Yes	3 Years
ABC Energy	$1,000	0%	AAA	$208.3	20	Yes	NA
TransPower	$1,000	10%	AA	$1092.0	20	Yes	5 Years
Telco Utilities	$1,000	11%	AA	$1206.4	30	No	5 Years

Questions:

1. How should Jill go about explaining the relationship between coupon rates and bond prices? Why do the coupon rates for the various bonds vary so much?

2. How are the ratings of these bonds determined? What happens when the bond ratings get adjusted downwards?

3. During the presentation one of the clients is puzzled why some bonds sell for less than their face value while others sell for a premium. She asks whether the discount bonds are a bargain? How should Jill respond?

4. What does the term "yield to maturity" mean and how is it to be calculated?

5. What is the difference between the "nominal" and effective yields to maturity for each bond listed in Table 1? Which one should the investor use when deciding between corporate bonds and other securities of similar risk? Please explain.

6. Jill knows that the call period and its implications will be of particular concern to the audience. How should she go about explaining the effects of the call provision on bond risk and return potential.

7. How should Jill go about explaining the riskiness of each bond? Rank order the bonds in terms of their relative riskiness.

8. One of Jill's best clients poses the following question, " If I buy 10 of each of these bonds, reinvest any coupons received at the rate of 5% per year and hold them until they mature, what will my realized return be on each bond investment?" How should she proceed?

9

Application of Stock Valuation Methods

How Low Can It Go?

Dwayne sat at his desk wondering what he should do. Having opted for early retirement, six months ago, he knew that he needed to make some changes in the way his investment portfolio was structured. However, being primarily focused on science during his career, he had a fairly limited knowledge of stock selection and portfolio management. One thing was certain, though, Dwayne had an eagerness to learn and that's exactly what he planned to do during his appointment with his broker, Jonathan Price.

Dwayne Stevenson, aged 58, had joined the Pharmacopia Company approximately thirty years ago, as a post-doctoral researcher in the field of immunology. His strong work ethic and knowledge of science enabled him to progress steadily along the research track of the company. He won a number of awards and earned many promotions along the way. Five years ago, Dwayne earned the coveted title of

"Research 5 Scientist" enjoyed by only 4 other individuals in the corporation. One of the main advantages of gaining the "Research 5" status was that he was given stock options as part of his remuneration package. At that time, shares of Pharmacopia (PCU) were trading at $30 per share. The company had annual sales in excess of $5 billion and the sales and earnings growth forecasts for the next few years were good. The company had applied for Food and Drug Administration (FDA) approval for two highly promising drugs and had a number of others in the pipeline.

However, as luck would have it, about 3 years later, the firm suffered a few setbacks. The FDA did not approve a couple of its applications and Pharmacopia was being investigated by the Environmental Protection Agency (EPA) for possible dumping violations. Besides, the patents on two of its best selling drugs expired and the generic versions began to flood the market. Needless to say, the firm's sales began to suffer and profits began to shrink sending its stock price into a downward spiral. 'Downsizing' and cost cutting were buzzwords that could be heard throughout the firm and on Wall Street.

About a year later, Dwayne was offered the option to take early retirement, primarily because his project was one that had not gained FDA approval. The severance package offered by the company was too good to turn down so Dwayne opted for early retirement. Part of the retirement package included a significant amount of company stock, which was trading at $12 at the time.

As a result of having exercised stock options and his early-retirement package, Dwayne had accumulated over 100,000 shares of PCU's common stock. This caused his investment portfolio to not be well diversified and Dwayne knew that he needed to restructure it. With PUC's stock price having declined to $8 per share in recent months, Dwayne wondered whether he should sell the stock or hold it until it reached a better price. Having had very little financial and investment training, Dwayne contacted his broker, Jonathan Price, for some advice. His main question to Jonathan was, "How low can it go?"

Jonathan told him to hold on to the stock because his calculations showed that it was significantly undervalued at $8 per share and should rise to about $28 per share in a few months. He felt that the company was having temporary regulatory problems and should be able to weather the storm quite well. He said that the intrinsic value of the stock, in his opinion, was in the range of $10 - $20. Not convinced, Dwayne asked him to explain how he arrived at that range. Jonathan replied that he used alternate forms of the dividend discount model, to which Dwayne responded, "Dividend what?" Jonathan realized that he would have to give Dwayne a primer on stock valuation and set up an appointment for the following week.

In preparation for the appointment, Jonathan prepared Table 1 showing the sales, net income, earnings per share, and dividend per share data for the prior 10-year period. In addition, he estimated the firm's beta and noted down the risk-free rate, market risk premium, and the expected growth rate of the pharmaceutical industry (shown in Table 2). Jonathan knew that he would have to keep his explanations simple, yet convincing, and expected to be faced with many difficult questions.

Table 1

Pharmacopia Company
Key Financial Data for Prior 10-year Period
(in $ millions except EPS, DPS)

Year	Sales	Net Income	EPS	DPS
1992	3,000	150	1.50	0.6
1993	3,200	160	1.60	0.64
1994	4,000	200	2.00	0.80
1995	4,400	220	2.20	0.88
1996	4,800	240	2.40	0.96
1997	5,000	250	2.50	1.00
1998	5,200	260	2.60	1.04
1999	5,100	255	2.55	1.02
2000	4,900	245	2.45	0.98
2001	4,700	235	2.35	0.94

Table 2

Systematic Risk, Industry Growth Rate, Interest Rates

Beta	1.1	
30-year Treasury Bond Yield		5.1%
Expected Market Risk Premium	9%	
Industry Average Growth rate		
10%		

Questions:

1. How should Jonathan describe the rationale of the dividend discount model (DDM) and demonstrate its use in calculating the justifiable price of common stock?

2. Being a researcher, Dwayne asked Jonathan a key question, "How did you estimate the growth rates used in applying the model?" Using the data given in Tables 1 and 2 explain how Jonathan should respond.

3. What is the rationale of the required rate of return that Jonathan used and how did he estimate it?

4. "What other variations of the DDM can one use and why?" asked Dwayne. What should Jonathan's response be?

5. "Why are you using dividends and not earnings per share, Jonathan?" asked Dwayne. What do you think Jonathan would have said?

6. Dwayne wondered whether Pharmacopia's preferred stock would be a better investment than its common stock, given that it was paying a dividend of $1.5 and trading at a price of $15. He asked Jonathan to explain to him the various features of preferred stock, how it differed from common stock and corporate bonds, and the method that could be used for estimating its value.

10

Estimating Cash Flow - New Project Analysis

The Lazy Mower: Is It Really Worth It?

If there was one thing the folks at Creative Products Company (CPC) knew well, it was how to come up with useful and unique products in the midst of economic adversity. With current year revenues considerably lower and profit margins shrinking due to severe price competition, the firm's engineers had been pushed really hard to develop a proto-type of a useful, and hopefully, highly profitable "unique" product. Then, last month, the design team unveiled a fully-tested, proto-type of their latest innovation, the remote-controlled" lawn mower, nick-named the "The Lazy Mower."

Surveys of retailers and customers, conducted by the marketing department, indicated that demand would be excellent, provided the price was lower than a tractor. The testing and development took almost 3 years and the final product passed all safety hazard tests with flying colors. After the unveiling, the product was exhibited at various home shows nationwide and received raving reviews. Full production had not yet started, however, because there had been a change in CEOs and the new CEO was highly conservative.

Before being given the "go ahead" to go into full-scale production of the Lazy Mower, the design team had to present a detailed feasibility study to the Capital Investment Committee, which was chaired by the Vice President of Finance, Gary Lester. As was typical in a major undertaking of this type, the proposal had to include detailed cost and revenue estimates with sufficient documentation to substantiate the numbers.

Having been involved with more than a few of these kinds of proposals before, the head of the Design team, Dave Crotte, knew that he had better take every possible factor into consideration and be prepared for a tough and demanding question and answer session at the next committee meeting. Luckily for Dave, his assistant, Richard Snow, who had recently earned his Chartered Financial Analyst (CFA) designation, was an experienced and dependable employee. Prior to being hired by CPC three years ago, Rick had worked for another large engineering company for over 10 years. "Richard, we have to dot all the "i's" and cross all the "t's" on this one!" said Dave. "Or else, the big guys are going to tear us apart, coz we're talking major dollars here. Their main question is going to be, IS IT REALLY WORTH IT?"

So Dave and Rick began collecting the necessary information. They knew that to have a comprehensive feasibility study they would have to include the following:

1. Pro Forma statements showing expected annual revenues, variable costs, fixed costs, and net cash flows over the economic life of the project with appropriate supporting documentation;
2. Break-Even Analysis;
3. Sensitivity of the cash flows to alternative scenarios of sales growth and profit margins;

Based on the data provided by the Marketing department, they prepared Table 1, showing the expected unit sales of the Lazy Mower over its 10-year economic life and the expected selling price per unit. Note that the price of $700 per unit was estimated to gradually drop to $600 per unit over the 10-year period reflecting competitive pressures. Depreciation for this project was based on the 7-year MACRS rates as shown in Table 2. The cost of equipment, including shipping, handling, and installation, was estimated at $30 million. It was estimated that after 10 years, the equipment and tools could be sold for $3 million.

The manufacturing would be done in an unused plant of the firm. Similar plant locations could be leased for $10,000 per month. Fixed costs were estimated to be $2,000,000 per year while variable production costs per unit were expected to be $400. To get the project underway, additional inventory of $500,000 would be required. The company would increase its accounts payable by $700,000 and its accounts receivable by $1,000,000. Dave and Rick estimated that each year there after, the net working capital of the firm would amount to 5% of sales. The weighted average cost of capital was calculated to be 18%. Interest expenses on debt raised to fund the project were estimated to be $400,000 per year. The company's tax rate was 34%.

Table 1

Projected Unit Sales and Price for Lazy Mower

Year	Unit Sales	Unit Price
1	20,000	$700
2	24,000	700
3	28,800	700
4	28,000	650
5	26,000	650
6	26,000	650
7	25,500	650
8	25,000	600
9	24,500	600
10	24,000	600

Table 2

Modified ACRS Depreciation Allowances

Year	3-Year	5-Year	7-Year
1	33.33%	20.00%	14.29%
2	44.44	32.00	24.49
3	14.82	19.20	17.49
4	7.41	11.52	12.49
5		11.52	8.93
6		5.76	8.93
7			8.93
8			4.45

Questions:

1.   Prepare a Pro Forma Statement showing the annual cash flows resulting from the Lazy Mower project.

2.   Use a scenario analysis to show how the cash flows would change if the sales forecasts were 15% worse (Pessimistic) and 15% better (Optimistic) than the stated forecast (base).

3.   Realizing that the CIC will demand some kind of sensitivity analyses, how should Dave and Rick prepare their report? Which variables or inputs are obvious ones that need to be analyzed using multiple values? Explain by performing suitable calculations.

4.   How should the interest expenses be treated? Explain.

5.   Using the base case estimates calculate the cash, accounting, and financial breakeven of the Lazy Mower project. Interpret each one.

6.   Let's say that the company had spent $500,000 in developing the prototype of the Lazy Mower. How should Dave and Rick treat this item in their report? Please explain.

7.   Calculate the IRR of the project. Based on your calculations what would you recommend? Why?

8.   How sensitive is the Net Present Value of the project to the cost of capital?

9.   Calculate the operating leverage entailed by this project. What does it indicate?

10.   What other types of contingency planning should Dave and Rick include to make the report comprehensive? Please explain the relevance of each suggestion.

11

Replacement Project Analysis

If the Coat Fits Wear It

The Innovative Sporting Goods Company (ISGC) was founded in 1975 in Cambridge, MA. Its founder, Andy Pratt, a mechanical engineer, had developed a sound technique of making baseball bats. Under his leadership, the company had gained national reputation. Recently, however, a new machine had been developed in the industry, which would allow manufacturers to coat the aluminum baseball bats with a special compound giving them a satin finish and making them more durable and powerful. The prototype had been presented to the respective regulatory authorities and had been approved. Upon Andy's request, Douglas Adams, the head of the design group, had tested the new product and researched the relevant cost and production process issues that a machine replacement would entail.

Doug reported that besides the initial price tag of $350,000 for one of these machines, users would have to incur shipping, handling, and installation costs of $4500 and annual fixed operating costs of about $20,000 per machine. Currently, the company incurs fixed operating costs of $28,000 for it's coating and finishing process. Initial marketing survey results indicated that the company would be able to increase sales of its newly designed baseball bats by about 15% in the first year of introduction and thereafter at a rate of 5% per year compared with forecasted sales growth of 2% per year for the current type of baseball bats. During the most recent year, ISGC sold 220,000 baseball bats at an average price of $12.50 per unit. The newly designed bat was expected to sell for $13 per unit.

Material, labor, general, and administrative costs were expected to remain constant at $10 per unit. The increased sales and production requirements would entail an increase in accounts receivables of $54,000, an increase in accounts payables of 30,000, and an increase in inventory of $ 20,000. It was assumed that any increase in net working capital would be recovered at the end of the useful life of the machine, which was estimated to be 10 years. The existing machine was purchased 5 years ago for $225,000. The depreciation on the existing machine was being calculated using a 15-year straight-line schedule with the assumption of no residual salvage value. The machine had a current market value of $100,000, and an expected market value of $10,000 after 10 more years of use. The new machine was expected to last for ten years -- the same as the remaining life of the old machine. The new machine would qualify as a 5-year class life asset under MACRS depreciation rates (see Table 1) and was expected to have a market value of approximately $20,000 at the end of its economic life. ISGC'S marginal tax rate was 34% and its weighted average cost of capital was estimated at 15%. Part of the cost of replacing the existing machine would be financed by a bank loan that would require an annual interest expense of 10% on the outstanding balance.

Andy knows that the new technology is the way to go. However, being cautious and conservative by nature, he does not want to implement changes that would be financially detrimental to his company. After all, he has worked too hard to let it all slip away by making lousy financial decisions. Andy has long believed in the age-old saying, " If the coat fits wear it."

Table 1

Depreciation Schedule				
Modified Accelerated Cost Recovery System				
Recovery Period Class				
Year	**3-Year**	**5-Year**	**7-Year**	**10-Year**
1	33.0%	20.0%	14.3%	10.0%
2	45.0%	32.0%	24.5%	18.0%
3	15.0%	19.2%	17.5%	14.4%
4	7.0%	11.5%	12.5%	11.5%
5	0.0%	11.5%	8.9%	9.2%
6	0.0%	5.8%	8.9%	7.4%
7	0.0%	0.0%	8.9%	6.6%
8	0.0%	0.0%	4.5%	6.6%
9	0.0%	0.0%	0.0%	6.5%
10	0.0%	0.0%	0.0%	6.5%
11	0.0%	0.0%	0.0%	3.3%
Total	100.0%	100.0%	100.0%	100.0%

Questions:

1. Your supervisor, Vic Gonzales, has asked you to prepare a capital budgeting report indicating whether ISGC should replace the existing machine or not. Indicate how would you proceed (without making any calculations)?

2. Explain the relevance of incremental cash flows, sunk costs, and incidental costs in the context of this case.

3. As is often the case, the marketing department has overestimated the annual sales growth. How can more conservative and realistic estimates be generated? How can these estimates be incorporated into the analysis so as to arrive at a good and well-justified decision?

4.   What are the relevant factors and items to be considered when estimating the initial outlay? Calculate the initial outlay for this replacement project.

5.   How are the interim cash flows to be computed for the productive life of the new machinery? How is depreciation to be accounted for?

6.   As a shrewd financial analyst you observe that the net working capital of the firm has typically been about 20% of the annual revenues. How would you incorporate this observation into the analysis?

7.   How should the annual interest expenses on the bank loan be handled? Explain.

8.   What is the relevance of the terminal year cash flow? Which factors must be considered when estimating the terminal year cash flow?

9.   After looking at the data provided by Vic, you realize that the revenue and cost figures have not been adjusted for inflation. If inflation was expected to be at least 3% per year, what effect would this have on your analysis? Adjust the data and recalculate the relevant cash flows.

10. What recommendation would you make to Vic regarding the replacement of the old coating machine? Explain.

11. If the new machine has an economic life of 15 years while the current machine has a life of only 10 years, how would the capital budgeting analysis have to be adjusted? Please explain by performing the necessary calculations.

12

Comparison of Capital Budgeting Techniques

The Dilemma at Day-Pro

The Day-Pro Chemical Corporation, established in 1995, has managed to earn a consistently high rate of return on its investments. The secret of its success has been the strategic and timely development, manufacturing, and marketing of innovative products that have been used in various industries. Currently, the management of the company is considering the manufacture of a thermosetting resin as packaging material for electronic products. The Company's Research and Development teams have come up with two alternatives: an epoxy resin, which would have a lower startup cost, and a synthetic resin, which would cost more to produce initially but would have greater economies of scale. At the initial presentation, the project leaders of both teams presented their cash flow projections and provided sufficient documentation in support of their proposals. However, since the products are mutually exclusive, the firm can only fund one proposal.

In order to resolve this dilemma, Mike Matthews, the Assistant Treasurer, and a recent MBA from a prestigious mid-western university, has been assigned the task of analyzing the costs and benefits of the two proposals and presenting his findings to the board of directors. Mike knows that this will be an uphill task, since the board members are not all on the same page when it comes to financial concepts. The Board has historically had a strong preference for using rates of return as its decision criteria. On occasions it has also used the payback period approach to decide between competing projects. However, Mike is convinced that the net present value (NPV) method is least flawed and when used correctly will always add the most value to a company's wealth.

After obtaining the cash flow projections for each project (see Tables 1 & 2), and crunching out the numbers, Mike realizes that the hill is going to be steeper than he thought. The various capital budgeting techniques, when applied to the two series of cash flows, provide inconsistent results. The project with the higher NPV has a longer payback period, as well as a lower Accounting Rate of Return (ARR) and Internal Rate of Return (IRR). Mike scratches his head, wondering how he can convince the Board that the IRR, ARR, and Payback Period can often lead to incorrect decisions.

Table 1

	Year 0	Year 1	Year 2	Year 3	Year 4	Year 5
Synthetic Resi						
Net Income		$150,000	$200,000	$300,000	$450,000	$500,000
Depreciation						
(Straight-line)		$200,000	$200,000	$200,000	$200,000	$200,000
Net Cash Flow	-$1,000,000	$350,000	$400,000	$500,000	$650,000	$700,000

Table 2

Epoxy Resin	Year 0	Year 1	Year 2	Year 3	Year 4	Year 5
Net Income		$440,000	$240,000	$140,000	$40,000	$40,000
Depreciation (Straight-line)		$160,000	$160,000	$160,000	$160,000	$160,000
Net Cash Flow	-$800,000	$600,000	$400,000	$300,000	$200,000	$200,000

Questions:

1. Calculate the Payback Period of each project. Explain what argument Mike should make to show that the Payback Period is not appropriate in this case.

2. Calculate the Discounted Payback Period (DPP) using 10% as the discount rate. Should Mike ask the Board to use DPP as the deciding factor? Explain.

3. If management prefers to have a 40% accounting rate of return, which project would be accepted? What is wrong with this decision?

4. Calculate the two projects' IRR. How should Mike convince the Board that the IRR measure could be misleading.

5. Calculate the NPV profiles for the two projects and explain the relevance of the crossover point. How should Mike convince the Board that the NPV method is the way to go?

6. Explain how Mike can show that the Modified Internal Rate of Return is the more realistic measure to use in the case of mutually exclusive projects.

7. Calculate the Profitability Index for each proposal. Can this measure help to solve the dilemma? Explain.

8. In looking over the documentation prepared by the two project teams, it appears to you that the synthetic resin team has been somewhat more conservative in its revenue projections than the epoxy resin team. What impact might this have on your analysis?

9. In looking over the documentation prepared by the two project teams, it appears to you that the synthetic resin technology would require extensive development before it could be implemented whereas the epoxy resin technology is available off-the-shelf." What impact might this have on your analysis?

13

Risk and Return

Flirting with Risk

When Mary Owens' husband, Ralph, passed away about three months ago he left behind a small fortune, which he had accumulated by living a very thrifty life and by investing in common stocks. Ralph had worked as an engineer for a surgical instruments manufacturer for over 30 years and had taken full advantage of the company's voluntary retirement savings plan. However, instead of buying a diversified set of investments he had invested his money into a few high growth companies. Over time his investment portfolio had grown to about $900,000 being primarily comprised of the stocks of 3 companies. He was very fortunate that his selections turned out to be good ones and after numerous stock-splits the prices of the three companies had appreciated significantly over time.

Mary, on the other hand was a very conservative and cautious person. She had devoted her life to being a stay-home mom and had raised their two kids into fine adults, each of whom had a fairly successful career. Jim, 28, had followed in Ralph's footsteps. In addition to being gainfully employed as an engineer, he was pursuing an MBA at a prestigious business school. Annette, 26, was completing her residency at a major metropolitan hospital. Although Mary and Ralph had enjoyed a wonderful married life, it was Ralph who managed almost all the financial affairs of their family. Mary, like many spouses of their generation, preferred to focus on other family matters.

It was only after Ralph's passing on that Mary realized how unprepared she was for the complex decisions that have to be made when managing one's wealth. Upon the advice of her close friend, Agnes, Mary decided to call the broker's office and request that her account be turned over to Bill May, the firm's senior financial advisor. Agnes, a widow herself, had been very happy with Bill's advice and professionalism. He had helped her rebalance and re-allocate her portfolio with the result that her portfolio's value had steadily increased over the years without much volatility.

At their first meeting, Bill examined the Owens' portfolio and was shocked at how narrowly focused its composition had been. In fact, just during the past year --due to the significant drop in the technology sector --the portfolio had lost almost 30% of its value. "Ralph, certainly liked to flirt with risk," said Bill. "The first thing we are going to have to do is diversify your portfolio and lower its beta. As it stands you could make a lot of money if the technology sector takes off, but the reverse scenario could be devastating. I am sure you will agree with me that given your status in life you do not need to bear this much of risk." Mary shrugged her shoulders and looked blankly at Bill. "Diversify...Beta... what are you talking about? These terms are new to me and so confusing. You are right, Bill, I don't need the high risk but can you explain to me how the risk level of my portfolio can be lowered?" Bill realized right away that Mary needed a primer on the risk-return tradeoff and on portfolio management. Accordingly, he scheduled another appointment for later that week and prepared the following exhibit to demonstrate the various nuances of risk, expected return, and portfolio management.

Exhibit 1

		Expected Rate of Return				
Scenario	Probability	Treasury Bill	Index Fund	Utility Company	High-Tech Company	Counter-Cyclical Company
Recession	20%	5%	-10%	6%	-25%	20%
Near Recession	20%	5%	-6%	7%	-20%	16%
Normal	30%	5%	12%	9%	15%	12%
Near Boom	10%	5%	15%	11%	25%	-9%
Boom	20%	5%	20%	14%	35%	-20%

Questions:

1. Imagine you are Bill. How would you explain to Mary the relationship between risk and return of individual stocks?

2. Mary has no idea what beta means and how it is related to the required return of the stocks. Explain how you would help her understand these concepts.

3. How should Bill demonstrate the meaning and advantages of diversification to Mary?

4. Using a suitable diagram explain how Bill could use the security market line to show Mary which stocks could be undervalued and which may be overvalued?

5. During the presentation. Mary asks Bill " Let's say I choose a well diversified portfolio, what effect will interest rates have on my portfolio? How should Bill respond?

6. Should Bill take Mary out of investing in stocks and preferably put all her money in fixed-income securities? Explain.

7. Mary tells Bill, "I keep hearing stories about how people have made thousands of dollars by following their brokers' "hot tips." Can you give me some hot tips regarding undervalued stocks?" How should Bill respond?

8. If Mary decided to invest her money equally in high-tech and counter-cyclical stocks, what would her portfolio's expected return and risk level be? Are these expectations realistic? Please explain.

9. What would happen if Mary were to put 70% of her portfolio in the High-Tech stock and 30% in the Index Fund? Would this combination be better for her? Explain.

10. Based on these calculations what do you think Bill should propose as a possible portfolio combination for Mary?

14

Real Options and Capital Budgeting

I Wish I Had a Crystal Ball

Mark Wise could feel the pressure as he walked into the executive boardroom with his briefcase containing the data and slides pertaining to his latest proposal. The last couple of years had not been very good for him. Two of the projects that he had recommended for investment ended up having to be abandoned, and one that he had turned down ended up being a winner for one of the firm's main competitors. Mark knew that this was going to be a long meeting.

Mark, the product development manager for Mid-West Pharmaco Corporation, had joined the firm about 7 years ago. With an undergraduate degree in Chemistry and an MBA in Finance from a nationally recognized university, Mark, had been fairly successful in his professional career. Prior to working at Mid-West Pharmaco, Mark had been responsible for the launching of three highly successful drugs at another pharmaceutical company. It didn't take long for the headhunters to find him and shortly thereafter Mid-West Pharmaco made him an offer that was too good to refuse. At Mid-West, however, his track record was not as good. Three of his last five recommendations had cost the company some serious money and Mark knew that this time his job was on the line. He remembered how last night as he was putting the finishing touches to his presentation he kept saying to himself, **"I wish I had a crystal ball."**

The Mid-West Pharmaco Corporation, headquartered in Rockford, Illinois, was a fairly large pharmaceutical company that had a number of patented drugs under its belt. However, two of the patents of its best sellers had recently expired and the generic drug manufacturers were chipping away at its profits. Although the company had employed a number of excellent research scientists and technicians, and had a number of projects in the pipeline, the stock price had tumbled during the past year mainly due to the lackluster performance of a couple of its drugs that were expected to be block-busters. One of the major problems facing the pharmaceutical industry was the difficulty of making reasonably accurate risk/return projections, primarily stemming from the requirement of obtaining approval from the Food and Drug Administration (FDA) prior to marketing the drug. In the past, overconfidence on part of the folks in marketing and business planning had resulted in some rash and unprofitable decisions.

The Vision Research division of the company had developed a new drug, nicknamed, ClearVision, for the cure of myopia, which had shown tremendous promise in preliminary tests. The project leader, Sam Grady, was confident that the drug would revolutionize the world of ophthalmology. Mark had carefully analyzed the cost and revenue estimates that were presented to him (see Table 1). Based on the figures provided by the project team, Mark calculated the Net Present Value and Internal Rate of Return of the project. The numbers looked good. However, Mark had learnt from his earlier mistakes, that one cannot take cost and revenue estimates at face value. Accordingly, he prepared a scenario analysis of the "ClearVision" project by varying the marketing costs, testing costs, and market share to reflect the best case, worst case, and most likely case scenarios (see Table 2) "My analysis shows that the outcome of the project depends heavily on the degree of market penetration achieved by the firm," said Mark. "A slight drop in market share accompanied by a 10% increase in testing and marketing costs (Worst Case) tends to make the NPV negative. However, if we can keep the testing and marketing costs at $110 million or less and have a market penetration of 8% or more, the project will be profitable. I think given the strategic nature of this product, we should go ahead with it. I have a strong feeling that this one's a winner.

As soon as he had finished his presentation, Barry Richards, the youngest director on the board, raised the question, "Have you considered the possibility that we may not get FDA approval within one year, if at all? What do we do then?" Mark's worst fears had come true. He had seen this coming. "That's a risk we have to live with, Barry." He said. But I am willing to go back and rework the numbers assuming a 1- or 2- year delay in getting FDA approval. Will that help?" "It certainly will," said Barry, "I guess that's the best we can do since we don't have a crystal ball!"

Questions:

1.   What is a real option? Explain how this project can be viewed as a real option.

2.   If you were a director on Mid-West Pharmaco's board would you agree with Mark's analysis? Explain.

3.   How would the numbers turn out after taking into consideration the contingency that the drug may not be sold until year 2 or 3 due to delay in getting FDA approval?

4.   What are strategic options? What kind of strategic options would apply in this case?

Table 1

Cash Flows, NPV and IRR Analysis of 'ClearVision' Project (Most Likely Case)**

(millions)		0	1	2	3	4	5	6	7	8	9	10
Development Costs		$-80											
Testing Costs		$-10											
Marketing Costs		$-100											
Total Cost		$-190											
Population with myopia		40	40.8	41.6	42.4	43.3	44.2	45.0	45.9	46.9	47.8	48.8
Growth rate of population with myopia	2%											
Cash Flow on dosages sold:												
Market share	8%		3.26	3.33	3.40	3.46	3.53	3.60	3.68	3.75	3.82	3.90
Net Cash Flow if approved @ $12/customer	$12	$-190	$39.17	$39.95	$40.75	$41.57	$42.40	$43.24	$44.11	$44.99	$45.89	$46.81
IRR	18%											
Cost of Capital	12%											
NPV	$42.81											

**Assumes 10-year patent protection

Table 2
**Scenario-based Assumptions regarding Cost Estimates and
Market Share for ClearVision Project**

	Testing Costs	Marketing Costs	Market Share
Worst Case Scenario	$11 million	$110 million	6%
Most Likely Case Scenario	$10 million	$100 million	8%
Best Case Scenario	$9 million	$ 90 million	10%

Table 3

Scenario Analysis of 'ClearVision' Project

	(millions) Worst Case	(millions) Most Likely	(millions) Best Case
Development Costs	$ (80)	$ (80)	$ (80)
Testing Costs	$ (11)	$ (10)	$ (9)
Initial Marketing Costs	$ (110)	$ (100)	$ (90)
Total Cost	$ (201)	$ (190)	$ (179)
Population with myopia	40	40	40
Growth rate of population with myopia	2%	2%	2%
Cash Flow on dosages sold:			
Market share	6%	8%	10%
Discounted Net Cash Flows (if approved) @$12/customer for Years 1 through 10.	$ 181	$ 233	$ 285
IRR	9.28%	17.68%	26.06%
Cost of Capital	12%	12%	12%
NPV	$ (20)	$ 43	$106

15

Determining the Cost of Capital

Better Late Than Never

Oceantech Corporation, a Chesapeake, VA based company, was incorporated in 1991. The corporation, which was privately owned at that time, was founded by Ralph Torrence, III after his retirement from NorshipCo. Oceantech was originally designed to provide ship repair services and quickly earned a Department of Defense (DOD) certified Alteration Boat Repair (ABR) designation. Among its specialties were structural welding, piping system installation and repairs, electrical, painting, rigging, machinery and dry-dock work, as well as custom sheet metal fabrication. Other divisions of Oceantech included, Habitability Installation, Industrial Contracting, and Alteration/Installation Teams (AIT). With its initial success and good return on investment the firm opened and operated facilities in California, New Jersey, Florida, Maryland, Pennsylvania and Washington.

In 1995, the company went public and its initial public offering was very successful. The stock price had risen from its initial value of $10 to its current level of $25 per share. There were currently 5 million shares outstanding. In 1997, the company issued 30-year bonds at par, with a face value of $1000 and a coupon rate of 10% per year, and managed to raise $40 million for expansion. Currently, the AA-rated bonds had 25 years left until maturity and were being quoted at 97.5% of par.

Over the past year, Oceantech utilized a new method for fabricating composite materials that the firm had developed. In June of last year, management established the Advanced Materials Group (AM Group), which was dedicated to pursuing this technology. The firm recruited Howard Sloan, a senior engineer, to head the AM Group. Howard also had an MBA from a prestigious university under his belt.

Upon joining Oceantech, Howard realized that most projects were being approved on a "gut feel" approach. There were no formal acceptance criteria in place. Up until then, the company had been lucky in that most of its projects had been well selected and it had benefited from good relationships with clients and suppliers. "This has to change," said Howard to his assistant Roseanne, "we can't possibly be this lucky forever. We need to calculate the firm's hurdle rate and use it in future." Roseanne Keane, who had great admiration for her boss replied, "Yes, Howard, why don't I crunch out the numbers and give them to you within the next couple of days?" " That sounds great, Roseanne," said Howard, "This should have been done a long time ago, but as most things go it's better late than never!"

As Roseanne began looking at the financial statements, she realized that she was going to have to make some assumptions. First, she assumed that new debt would cost about the same as the yield on outstanding debt and would have the same rating. Second, she assumed that the firm would continue raising capital for future projects by using the same target proportions as determined by the book values of debt and equity (see Table 1 for recent balance sheet). Third, she assumed that the equity beta (1.2) would be the same for all the divisions. Fourth, she assumed that the growth rates of earnings and dividends would continue at their historical rate (see Table 2 for earnings and dividend history). Fifth, she assumed that the corporate tax rate would be 40%, and finally, she assumed that the floatation cost for debt would be 10% of the issue price and that for equity would be 15% of selling price. The 1-year Treasury bill yield was 5% and the expected rate of return on the market portfolio was 12%.

Table 1

Oceantech Corporation Balance Sheet (*'000s*)			
Cash	5000	Accounts Payable	8000
Accounts Receivables	10000	Accruals	5000
Inventory	20000	Notes Payable	10000
Total Current Assets	*35000*	*Total Current Liabilities*	*23000*
Land&Buildings (net)	43000	Long-term debt	40000
Plant and Equipment (net)	45000	Common stock	
Total Fixed Assets	*88000*	(5 million shares outstanding)	50000
		Retained Earnings	10000
Total Assets	*123000*	*Total liabilities and shareholders' equity*	*123000*

Table 2

Oceantech Corporation Sales, Earnings, and Dividend History *('000s)*			
Year	Sales	Earnings per Share	Dividends per Share
1995	$24,000,000	$ 0.48	$ 0.19
1996	28,800,000	0.58	0.23
1997	36,000,000	0.72	0.29
1998	45,000,000	0.90	0.36
1999	51,750,000	1.04	0.41
2000	62,100,000	1.24	0.50
2001	74,520,000	1.49	0.60

Questions:

1. Why do you think Howard Sloan wants to estimate the firm's hurdle rate? Is it justifiable to use the firm's weighted average cost of capital as the divisional cost of capital? Please explain.

2. How should Roseanne go about figuring out the cost of debt? Calculate the firm's cost of debt.

3. Comment on Roseanne's assumptions as stated in the case. How realistic are they?

4. Why is there a cost associated with a firm's retained earnings?

5. How can Roseanne estimate the firm's cost of retained earnings? Should it be adjusted for taxes? Please explain?

6.   Calculate the firm's average cost of retained earnings.

7.   Can floatation costs be ignored in the analysis? Explain.

8.   How should Roseanne calculate the firm's hurdle rate? Calculate it and explain the various steps.

9.   Can Howard assume that the hurdle rate calculated by Roseanne would remain constant? Please explain.

16

Divisional Costs of Capital

We Are Not All Alike!

Sarah Anderson was at it again! It seemed like she made waves wherever she went. At her previous job, which incidentally was also with a Fortune 500 company, Sarah had successfully implemented a system of evaluating projects based on differential (risk-adjusted) hurdle rates. However, the change caused so much uproar and unpleasantness among divisional heads that Sarah knew her days at the job were numbered. Eventually she quit and given her sound credentials had no trouble finding another job.

At her current job as Vice President of Finance for American Modular Systems, Incorporated Sandra had to evaluate proposals that came in for funding from the firm's three product divisions, Defense, Consumer Products, and Industrial Supply. During her very first month at the job, she was presented with three funding requests, one from each department (see Table 1 for project cost and cash flow projections).

Being unclear as to what the policy was regarding the hurdle rate to be used in evaluating such projects, Sandra decided to calculate the company's weighted average cost of capital herself. After carefully analyzing the firm's financial statements and talking to the underwriters, Sandra estimated that the firm's weighted average cost of capital was around 14%.

When she consulted with her boss, Gary Pollock, she was pleased to learn that the firm had been using 14% recently as the hurdle rate for all project evaluations. What troubled her was the fact that like her previous employer, these folks too were not using differential hurdle rates for the three different divisions. "Here we go again," thought Sandra. "I should have asked about this at the interview. Oh well! I guess its too late now. I've got to do what I've got to do!"

American Modular Systems Inc., based in Charlotte, NC employed 5200 people at its three various corporate and manufacturing facilities. Its three divisions, Defense, Consumer Products, and Industrial Supply, were organized based on the type of products manufactured and the clientele served. The Defense Division accounted for around 55% of the sales volume, while the other two divisions split the balance. The company manufactured and supplied high quality storage units made from aluminum, plastic and wood. During the past few years the Defense division had done extremely well and was bringing in the majority of the firm's profits. However, as is typical of most defense contractors, there had been significant volatility in its sales and earnings figures over the past eight years. The Consumer Products, and Industrial Supply divisions had been far less volatile but their profit margins had been lower. Overall, though, the firm was fairly well diversified and its beta had been estimated at 1.5.

Sandra decided that she had better figure out a more logical method of adjusting the divisional hurdle rates, because she strongly believed that failure to do so would result in the firm making unwise capital budgeting decisions. Given her training and philosophy there was no way she was going to allow projects to be evaluated without due consideration being given to their respective volatilities. "We are not all alike," she said to her boss, Gary, "and we should not pretend to be. Don't you agree?" To her good luck, Gary agreed. So Sarah went to work.

The first thing she did was refer back to her notes from graduate school (they do come in handy sometimes, you know) and remembered that there were two ways she could go about doing the adjustment for differences in risk across corporate divisions. One way was to measure or collect the equity betas of comparable homogeneous companies and substitute those in place of the firm's overall beta when calculating the weighted average cost of capital. The other way was to simply adjust the firm's weighted average cost of capital up or down based on the relative variability of each division's sales and/or earnings. After doing some research on the Internet, Sandra decided against the first option because most of the firm's competitors were involved in multiple industry sectors. Accordingly, she decided to go ahead with the second alternative and requested the accounting department to provide her with quarterly sales data for the prior eight years broken down by divisions (Table 2). She decided to calculate the relative variability of each division's revenues with respect to that of the overall firm and accordingly adjust the firm's hurdle rate when evaluating proposals submitted by each department.

After doing some quick calculations, Sarah sent off emails to the Vice-Presidents of the three divisions setting up a time for a meeting. Somehow, Sarah knew that it was not going to be a pleasant meeting.

Table 1

Projected Costs, Lives, and Cash inflows of Divisional Proposals

Division	Cost	Life	Annual Net Cash Flow
Defense	$ (1,200,000)	5	$ 351,000
Consumer Products	$ (1,800,000)	6	$ 460,000
Industrial Relations	$ (1,500,000)	7	$ 348,000

Table 2

Divisional Breakdown of Quarterly Revenues

| | ------Quarterly Revenues------- | | | |
Quarter	Defense Products	Consumer Products	Industrial Products	Consolidated
1	3,000,000	1,700,000	1,600,000	6,300,000
2	3,150,000	1,751,000	1,648,000	6,549,000
3	3,307,500	1,803,530	1,697,440	6,808,470
4	3,472,875	1,857,636	1,748,363	7,078,874
5	3,646,519	1,913,365	1,800,814	7,360,698
6	3,828,845	1,970,766	1,854,839	7,654,449
7	3,943,710	2,029,889	1,910,484	7,884,083
8	4,062,021	2,090,786	1,967,798	8,120,605
9	4,183,882	2,153,509	2,026,832	8,364,223
10	4,309,398	2,218,114	2,087,637	8,615,150
11	4,438,680	2,284,658	2,150,266	8,873,604
12	4,571,841	2,353,198	2,214,774	9,139,813
13	4,708,996	2,423,794	2,281,217	9,414,007
14	4,850,266	2,496,507	2,349,654	9,696,427
15	4,995,774	2,571,403	2,420,144	9,987,320
16	4,745,985	2,648,545	2,492,748	9,887,278
17	5,030,744	2,728,001	2,567,530	10,326,276
18	5,231,974	2,809,841	2,644,556	10,686,371
19	5,441,253	2,894,136	2,723,893	11,059,282
20	5,658,903	2,980,960	2,805,610	11,445,473
21	5,885,259	3,070,389	2,889,778	11,845,426
22	6,120,670	3,162,501	2,976,471	12,259,642
23	6,365,496	3,257,376	3,065,765	12,688,638
24	6,620,116	3,355,097	3,157,738	13,132,952
25	6,951,122	3,455,750	3,284,048	13,690,920
26	7,298,678	3,559,422	3,382,569	14,240,670
27	7,663,612	3,666,205	3,484,046	14,813,864
28	8,046,793	3,776,191	3,623,408	15,446,392
29	8,449,132	3,889,477	3,732,111	16,070,720
30	8,871,589	4,006,161	3,844,074	16,721,824
31	9,315,168	4,126,346	3,959,396	17,400,911
32	9,780,927	4,250,137	4,078,178	18,109,241

Questions:

1. Using the data given in Table 2, determine the relative variability of each division's sales as compared to that of the consolidated firm. Which one is the riskiest and why?

2. Explain the process by which Sarah must have determined the hurdle rate for the entire company. The corporate tax rate was 40%, the yield on outstanding bonds was 10%, treasury bills were yielding 6% and the market risk premium was estimated at 9%. The company currently had 40% of its capital in the form of debt and the remaining in the form of common stock.

3. What is meant by the 'pure play' approach to estimating the required return on an investment?

4. Using Sarah's methodology of adjusting the firm's hurdle rate based on the relative variability of each division's sales in relation to that of the consolidated firm, calculate the divisional hurdle rates.

5. Comment on this methodology of estimating the divisional hurdle rates. Do you agree with it or not? Explain your answer.

6. Using the firm's overall weighted average cost of capital evaluate the three divisions' project proposals. What are your findings?

7. How do the decisions get affected when the divisional hurdle rates are used instead?

Economic Added Value:
Just Another Fad?

Nick Taylor could hardly wait to get back to his corporate headquarters in Philadelphia, Pennsylvania and share all the useful information that he had gathered on performance evaluation with his colleagues in the finance department. Nick was the Vice President of Finance at Philadelphia Manufacturing Company, a small sized firm with annual sales ranging from 4.5 million to 5 million dollars. The president of the company, Larry Brown, had recently heard about the effectiveness of the "economic value added (EVA)" measure of corporate performance at an executive summit and was interested in exploring its use for Philadelphia Manufacturing. He, therefore, asked Nick to attend a two-day workshop entitled "EVA – It really works!" hosted by Stern, Stewart, and Company at their headquarters in New York, NY.

Nick had been impressed by the quality of the presentations put on by the staff of Stern, Stewart and Company. One brochure in particular, he thought, summarized it all very well (see Exhibit 1). The list of companies that had adopted EVA as an evaluation measure was growing by leaps and bounds (see Exhibit 2). Furthermore, the empirical evidence linking the EVA performance yardstick with shareholder wealth creation was quite striking. In one of the studies done on 66 of Stern, Stewart's clients, it was reported that:

> "On average, investments in the shares of these companies produced 49% more wealth after five years than equal investments in shares of competitors with similar market capitalization. Companies that used the full Stern Stewart compensation architecture did even better. Investment in their shares produced 84% more wealth over five years than equal investments in their competitors. Overall, the Stern Stewart clients created some $116 billion more in market value than they would have if they had performed the same as their competitors."   (Stern, Stewart & Co.)

This finding, thought Nick, would be of particular interest to the folks at corporate headquarters, since plans were in the offing for taking the company public. He figured that he better prepare an outline for the finance staff to use when calculating the firm's EVA (see Exhibit 3). Nick knew that once the necessary financial details were worked out, the calculations would be easy to follow. He realized that being a small company, many of the adjustments suggested by Stern, Stewart & Company would not apply to Philadelphia Manufacturing. What would apply, though, would be the adjustment of $40,000 paid as salaries to the owners as part of net operating profits before taxes, rather than as an expenditure, since it was an investment in the future of the firm.

Nick glanced over the steps necessary to calculate EVA, which he had jotted down, and then at the latest annual financial statements of Philadelphia Manufacturing (see Tables 1 and 2). He realized that he would need to gather some more specific information before he could come up with a reasonably accurate measure of Philadelphia Manufacturing Company's EVA. He figured that he had better wait till he was back in Philadelphia.

Exhibit 1

WHAT IS EVA? **

Economic Value Added is the financial performance measure that comes closer than any other to capturing the true economic profit of an enterprise. EVA® also is the performance measure most directly linked to the creation of shareholder wealth over time. Stern Stewart & Co. guides client companies through the implementation of a complete EVA-based financial management and incentive compensation system that gives managers superior information - and superior motivation - to make decisions that will create the greatest shareholder wealth in any publicly owned or private enterprise.

EVA = Net Operating Profits After Taxes - ($Capital X Cost of Capital%)

Put most simply, EVA is net operating profit minus an appropriate charge for the opportunity cost of all capital invested in an enterprise. As such, EVA is an estimate of true "economic" profit, or the amount by which earnings exceed or fall short of the required minimum rate of return that shareholders and lenders could get by investing in other securities of comparable risk.

Profits the way shareholders count them
The capital charge is the most distinctive and important aspect of EVA. Under conventional accounting, most companies appear profitable but many in fact are not. As Peter Drucker put the matter in a *Harvard Business Review* article, "Until a business returns a profit that is greater than its cost of capital, it operates at a loss. Never mind that it pays taxes as if it had a genuine profit. The enterprise still returns less to the economy than it devours in resources...Until then it does not create wealth; it destroys it." EVA corrects this error by explicitly recognizing that when managers employ capital they must pay for it, just as if it were a wage.

By taking all capital costs into account, including the cost of equity, EVA shows the dollar amount of wealth a business has created or destroyed in each reporting period. In other words, EVA is profit the way shareholders define it. If the shareholders expect, say, a 10% return on their investment, they "make money" only to the extent that their share of after-tax operating profits exceeds 10% of equity capital. Everything before that is just building up to the minimum acceptable compensation for investing in a risky enterprise.

Aligning decisions with shareholder wealth

Stern Stewart developed EVA to help managers incorporate two basic principles of finance into their decision- making. The first is that the primary financial objective of any company should be to maximize the wealth of its shareholders. The second is that the value of a company depends on the extent to which investors expect future profits to exceed or fall short of the cost of capital. By definition, a sustained increase in EVA will bring an increase in the market value of a company. This approach has proved effective in virtually all types of organizations, from emerging growth companies to turnarounds. This is because the level of EVA isn't what really matters. Current performance already is reflected in share prices. It is the continuous improvement in EVA that brings continuous increases in shareholder wealth.

A financial measure line managers understand

EVA has the advantage of being conceptually simple and easy to explain to non-financial managers, since it starts with familiar operating profits and simply deducts a charge for the capital invested in the company as a whole, in a business unit, or even in a single plant, office or assembly line. By assessing a charge for using capital, EVA makes managers care about managing assets as well as income, and helps them properly assess the tradeoffs between the two. This broader, more complete view of the economics of a business can make dramatic differences.

Ending the confusion of multiple goals

Most companies use a numbing array of measures to express financial goals and objectives. Strategic plans often are based on growth in revenues or market share. Companies may evaluate individual products or lines of business on the basis of gross margins or cash flow. Business units may be evaluated in terms of return on assets or against a budgeted profit level. Finance departments usually analyze capital investments in terms of net present value, but weigh prospective acquisitions against the likely contribution to earnings growth. And bonuses for line managers and business-unit heads typically are negotiated annually and are based on a profit plan. The result of the inconsistent standards, goals, and terminology usually is incohesive planning, operating strategy, and decision making.

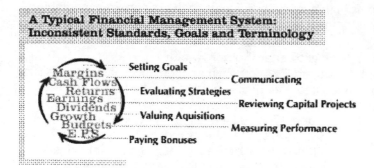

A Typical Financial Management System:
Inconsistent Standards, Goals and Terminology

Margins
Cash Flows
Returns
Earnings
Dividends
Growth
Budgets
E.P.S

Setting Goals
Communicating
Evaluating Strategies
Reviewing Capital Projects
Valuing Aquisitions
Measuring Performance
Paying Bonuses

EVA eliminates this confusion by using a single financial measure that links all decision making with a common focus: How do we improve EVA? EVA is the only financial management system that provides a common language for employees across all operating and staff functions and allows all management decisions to be modeled, monitored, communicated and compensated in a single and consistent way - always in terms of the value added to shareholder investment.

** Stern Stewart & Company (New York)

Exhibit 2

Sample list of companies using EVA as a performance measure*

ADC Telecommunications
Allied Holdings
Alltrista Corporation
American Saw & Manufacturing
The Andrew Jergens Company
Armstrong World Industries, Inc.
Ball Corp.
Bausch & Lomb
Best Buy Co., Inc
Boise Cascade Corp.
Bowater
Briggs & Stratton Corp.
C. H. Heist
California Microwave
Calmat
CalResources
Case Corp.
Centura Banks, Inc.
Cilcorp, Inc.
The Coca-Cola Co.
Columbus McKinnon Corp
Core Industries
Cowles Media Co.
Crane Co.
CSX Corp.
Chicago Extruded Metals, Inc.
Dresser Industries
Dun & Bradstreet Corp.
Echlin
EG&G, Inc.
Eli Lilly & Co.
ENTEX Information Services, Inc.
Equifax, Inc.
Federal-Mogul
Fleming Companies, Inc.
Furon Co.
Georgia-Pacific Corp.
Griffith Laboratories
Guidant Corp.
Herman Miller

Illinois Power Company
Insteel Industries, Inc.
International Multifoods
JCPenney
Johnson Worldwide Associates, Inc.
Kansas City Power & Light
Kao Corporation
KLLM Transport Services
Knape & Vogt Manufacturing
The Manitowoc Company
Material Sciences Corp.
Millennium Chemicals
Monsanto
Montana Power
The Moore Company
Noble Drilling
Olin Corp.
Premark International, Inc.
Pulte Corp.
R.P. Scherer
R.R. Donnelley
Rand McNally & Co.
Rubbermaid Inc.
Ryder System, Inc.
Sanifill Inc.
Shaw Industries
Silicon Valley Bancshares
Sprint
SPX Corp.
Standard Motor Products Inc.
Steelcase
Strategic Minerals Corp.
Toys R Us
A.M. Todd Group
U.S. Postal Service
W.C. Bradley
W.W. Grainger, Inc.
Waste Management
Weatherhead Industries
Webster Financial
Whirlpool

* Stern, Stewart & Co.

Exhibit 3

Steps involved in calculating EVA

1.   Review the company's income statement and balance sheet.

2.   Identify the company's capital sources and magnitudes ($Capital)
$Capital = Total Liabilities – Non-interest bearing liabilities.
Marketing Outlays, R&D costs and restructuring charges should be treated as capital investments (add back to NOPAT) rather than expenses.

3.   Determine the company's weighted average cost of capital (WACC).

WACC = (Cost of Debt * Weight of Debt in Capital Base)
+
(Cost of Equity * Weight of Equity in Capital Base)
Cost of Debt = Prime rate + Bank charges
Cost of Equity = 10 year bond yield + Risk Premium

4.   Calculate NOPAT

NOPAT = Net Income + Total Adjustments – Opportunity loss
of tax savings on
Adjustments

5.   Calculate EVA

EVA = NOPAT – (WACC*$Capital)

Table 1

Philadelphia Manufacturing Company

Income Statement (in thousands of dollars)

	2002	*2001*
Sales	4500	4700
CGS	2813	3008
SG&A expenses	1396	1504
Income from Operations	291	188
Other Income	0	0
EBIT	291	188
Interest expenses	35	30
Pretax income	256	158
Taxes(40%)	102	63
Net Income	154	95

Table 2

Philadelphia Manufacturing Company
Balance Sheet (in thousands of dollars)

	2002	2001
Cash	28	31
Accounts Receivable	879	842
Inventory	1121	977
Prepaid expenses	43	47
Other current assets	34	34
Total Current Assets	2105	1931
Computer equipment	100	92
Furniture and fixtures	20	21
Motor vehicles	39	34
Equipment	207	184
Other fixed assets	29	38
Total fixed assets	395	369
Total Assets	2500	2300
Accounts payable	671	645
Short-term debt	137	131
Accrued expenses	250	231
Total current liabilities	1058	1008
Long-term debt	653	603
Total Liabilities	1711	1611
Common stock	33	27
Retained Earnings	757	662
Total owners' equity	789	689
Total Liabilities & Owners' Equity	2500	2300

Questions:

1. Calculate and interpret Philadelphia Manufacturing Company's key liquidity, profitability, turnover, and leverage ratios. What do the ratios indicate?

2. Calculate the firm's NOPAT for both years. $40,000 of the owners' salary were considered to be a reinvestment for future growth of the firm.

3. What are the relative proportions of debt and equity in Philadelphia Manufacturing Company's capital structure?

4. Calculate the firm's cost of debt and equity. The prime rate is currently at 8% per year and the bank charges 2%. The company is in the 40% tax bracket. 10-year treasury notes are currently yielding 5% and the risk premium for Philadelphia's Equity is 7%.

5. Calculate the firm's EVA for both years. What does it indicate about the performance of the company?

6. Do your conclusions regarding the firm's performance, based on EVA, concur with those from the ratio analysis? Please explain.

7. What are the main advantages of using EVA as a performance evaluation measure?

18

Evaluating Project Risk

It's Better to Be Safe Than Sorry!

"It's amazing how much difference there is in the way proposals are presented at two different firms," said John Woods to his assistant, Pete Madsen, as he pointed to the stack of capital investment proposals piled on his desk. "We sure have our work cut out for us, Pete. I need you to collect some data for me as soon as possible. "

John Woods, had recently been hired as the Assistant Vice President of Finance of Mid-West Home Products. His past experience included a seven-year stint with another large consumer products firm. His career had been very successful, thus far, as he had gone from being a financial analyst to an Assistant Vice-President of Finance in a little over seven years. John, who held an undergraduate degree in Accounting and an MBA in Finance from nationally recognized business schools, preferred to follow a conservative policy when analyzing capital investment projects. Most of the projects that he had analyzed and got approved had turned out to be profitable for his former employers.

At a recent meeting of the Capital Investment Committee, which was the primary group responsible for approving proposals at Mid-West Home products, the five divisional managers had presented proposals that had cost estimates ranging from $250,000 to $750,000. All five proposals were shown to have positive net present values (NPVs) and fairly high internal rates of return (IRRs). Moreover, the cost and revenue figures seemed to be conservatively arrived at and all five proposals seemed to have good overall strategic value. However, upon careful deliberation and reflection, it was learned that the divisional managers had used the cost of debt as the minimum acceptable rate of return whilst evaluating their respective projects. The company had issued 20-year, 8% bonds, at par, last year and that rate was used as the hurdle rate under the assumption that additional funds could be raised at the same rate. There was considerable argument, confusion, and dissent at the meeting, when John brought up the issue of the firm's target capital structure and raised concerns that the hurdle rate for each project could vary depending on the total capital raised by the firm.

It was clear that there was a lack of full understanding and consensus about cost of capital issues among the 5 divisional managers, most of who did not have a finance background. Sensing that the meeting was going nowhere, the Chief Financial Officer, Sean Walker, said, "John, why don't you take these proposals, re-evaluate them based on appropriate discount rates, and present your recommendations at our next week's committee meeting. I'm sure you all will agree with me, that it is better to be safe than sorry!"

John started his analysis by listing the estimated cost, economic life, and internal rate of return of each proposal as shown in Table 1. He then collected data regarding the current prices, preferred dividend rate, retention ratio, and number of issues outstanding of the firm's bonds, preferred stock, and common stock (see Table 2). For this purpose, John referred to the latest balance sheet (shown in Table 3), income statement (see Table 4) and the Internet. A call to the firm's investment banker helped John obtain estimates of floatation costs that would apply based on the type of issue (see Table 5). As he crunched the numbers, John realized that he would need the following estimates:

1.   The firm's expected growth rate of sales, earnings and
        dividends;
2.   The expected return on the market index;
3.   The Treasury bill rate, and
4.   The firm's beta.

This is the list he passed on to his assistant, Pete.

Table 1

Project	Cost	IRR	Estimated Life	NPV @ 8%
			Project Information		
A	$ 500,000	20%	5 Years	$ 346,754.39
B	$ 750,000	12%	4 Years	$ 117,437.77
C	$ 250,000	16%	3 Years	$ 59,772.39
D	$ 600,000	25%	4 Years	$ 476,703.89
E	$ 400,000	15%	3 Years	$ 82,927.84

Table 2

Type	Par Value	Current Price	Number Outstanding
	Market Data Regarding Outstanding Securities		
10%, 20-Year Bonds	$1,000	$900	10,000
6% Preferred Stock	$10	$12	500,000
Common Stock	$1	$25	1,000,000

Table 3

Mid-West Home Products Last Year's Income Statement ('000s)	
Revenues	37500
Cost of Goods Sold	31875
Gross Profit	5625
Selling & Administration Expenses	1125
Depreciation	1000
Earnings Before Interest and Taxes	3500
Interest Expenses	887
Earnings Before Taxes	2613
Taxes (40%)	1045
Net Income	1,568
Preferred Dividends	300
Income Available for Common	1,268
Common Stock Dividends	508
Addition to Retained Earnings	760

Table 4

Mid-West Home Products Balance Sheet (000's)			
Current Assets	10,000	Current Liabilities	3000
Net Fixed Assets	75,000	Notes Payable	2000
		Long-term Debt (10,000 outstanding, Coupon Rate = 8%, Face Value = $1,000)	10000
		Preferrred Stock (500,000 outstanding, Dividend Rate = 6%, Par Value = $10)	50000
		Common Stock (1,000,000 outstanding)	20000
Total Assets	85,000	Total Liabilities & Shareholders' Equity	85000

Table 5

Floatation Cost Schedule	
Type of Security	*Issuance Cost*
Bonds	5%
Preferred Stock	10%
Common Stock	15%

Questions:

1.   What seems to be wrong with the way the NPV of each project has been calculated? Indicate without any calculations, how Pete and John should go about recalculating the projects' NPVs.

2.   Why does John need to know the retention rate of the firm? What impact will retained earnings have on the calculations?

3.   Why is the target capital structure of concern to John? How should it be determined?

4.   Pete collects the necessary data and prepares the Table 6 (shown below.) Accordingly, calculate the component costs of debt, preferred stock, and common stock. Will these costs be constant irrespective of the amount of capital raised? Please explain.

Table 6

Expected Growth Rate of Sales 25%
Expected Growth Rate of Earnings and Dividends 12%
Expected Return on the Market.. 5%
Treasury bill rate.. 6%
Expected retention rate 60%
Firm's Equity Beta... 1.2

5.   Develop and graph the Marginal Cost of Capital for the intended capital investments. Explain how the values are arrived at.

6.   Using the same graph as in #5, develop an Investment Opportunity Schedule using the data for the 5 proposals and accordingly indicate which combination of projects would be acceptable.

7.   Recalculate the NPVs of the 5 projects using the appropriate hurdle rate. Are the projects still acceptable? Please explain.

8.   Let's assume that the cash flows of Project B were 40% less risky than those of the other 4 projects –which were estimated to be of average risk. How would the evaluation process be affected and what would John have to do to make the appropriate recommendations?

19

Debt Versus Equity Financing

Look Before You Leverage

"Why do things have to be so complicated?" said Bob to Andrew, as he sat at his desk shuffling papers around. "I need you to come up with a convincing argument." Bob's company, Symonds Electronics, had embarked upon an expansion project, which had the potential of increasing sales by about 30% per year over the next 5 years. The additional capital needed to finance the project had been estimated at $5,000,000. What Bob was wondering about was whether he should burden the firm with fixed rate debt or issue common stock to raise the needed funds. Having had no luck with getting the board of directors to vote on a decision, Bob decided to call on Andrew Lamb, his Chief Financial Officer to shed some light on the matter.

Bob Symonds, the Chief Executive Officer of Symonds Electronics, established his company about 10 years ago in his hometown of Cincinnati, Ohio. After taking early retirement at age 55,

Bob felt that he could really capitalize on his engineering knowledge and contacts within the industry. Bob remembered vividly how easily he had managed to get the company up and running by using $3,000,000 of his own savings and a five-year bank note worth $2,000,000. He recollected how uneasy he had felt about that debt burden and the 14% per year rate of interest that the bank had been charging him. He remembered distinctly how relieved he had been after paying off the loan one year earlier than its five-year term, and the surprised look on the bank manager's face.

Business had been good over the years and sales had doubled about every 4 years. As sales began to escalate with the booming economy and thriving stock market, the firm had needed additional capital. Initially, Bob had managed to grow the business by using internal equity and spontaneous financing sources. However, about 5 years ago, when the need for financing was overwhelming, Bob decided to take the company public via an initial public offering (IPO) in the over-the-counter market. The issue was very successful and oversubscribed, mainly due to the superb publicity and marketing efforts of the investment underwriting company that Bob had excellent relations with. The company sold 1 million shares at $5 per share. The stock price had grown steadily over time and was currently trading at its book value of $15 per share.

When the expansion proposal was presented at last week's board meeting, the directors were unanimous about the decision to accept the proposal. Based upon the estimates provided by the marketing department, the project had the potential of increasing revenues by between 10% (Worst Case) and 50% (Best Case) per year. The internal rate of return was expected to far outperform the company's hurdle rate. Ordinarily, the project would have been started using internal and spontaneous funds. However, at this juncture, the firm had already invested all its internal equity into the business. Thus, Bob and his colleagues were hard pressed to make a decision as to whether long-term debt or equity should be the chosen method of financing this time around.

Upon contacting their investment bankers, Bob learned that they could issue 5-year notes, at par, at a rate of 10% per year. Conversely, the company could issue common stock at its current price of $15 per share. Being unclear about what decision to make, Bob put the question to a vote by the directors. Unfortunately, the directors were equally divided in their opinion of which financing route should be chosen. Some of the directors felt that the tax shelter offered by debt would help reduce the firm's overall cost of capital and prevent the firm's earnings per share from being diluted. However, others had heard about "homemade leverage" and would not be convinced. They were of the opinion that it would be better for the firm to let investors leverage their investments themselves. They felt that equity was the way to go since the future looked rather uncertain and being rather conservative, they were not interested in burdening the firm with interest charges. Besides, they felt that the firm should take advantage of the booming stock market.

Feeling rather frustrated and confused, Bob, decided to call upon his chief financial officer, Andrew Lamb, to resolve this dilemma. Andrew, had joined the company about two years ago. He held an MBA from a prestigious university and had recently completed his Chartered Financial Analysts' certification. Prior to joining Symonds, Andrew had worked at two other publicly traded manufacturing companies and had been successful in helping them raise capital at attractive rates, thereby lowering their cost of capital considerably.

Andrew knew that he was in for a challenging task. He felt, however, that this was a good opportunity to prove his worth to the company. In preparation of his presentation, he got the latest income statement and balance sheet of the firm (see Tables 1 and 2) and started crunching out the numbers. The title of his presentation read, "Look Before You Leverage!"

Table 1

Symonds Electronics Inc.			
Latest Balance Sheet			
Cash	1,000,000	Accounts Payable	3,000,000
Accounts Receivables	3,000,000	Accruals	2,000,000
Inventories	4,000,000		
Current Assets	8,000,000	Current Liabilities	5,000,000
Net Fixed Assets	12,000,000	Paid in Capital	5,000,000
		Retained Earnings	10,000,000
		Total Liabilities &	
Total Assets	20,000,000	Owner's Equity	20,000,000

Table 2

Symonds Electronics Inc.	
Latest Income Statement	
Sales	15,000,000
Cost of Goods Sold	10,500,000
Gross Profit	4,500,000
Selling and Adm. Exp	750,000
Depreciation	1,500,000
EBIT	2,250,000
Taxes (40%)	900,000
Net Income	1,350,000

Questions:

1. If Symonds Electronics Inc. were to raise all of the required capital by issuing debt, what would the impact be on the firm's shareholders?

2. What does "homemade leverage" mean? Using the data in the case explain how a shareholder might be able to use homemade leverage to create the same payoffs as achieved by the firm.

3. What is the current weighted average cost of capital of the firm? What effect would a change in the debt to equity ratio have on the weighted average cost of capital and the cost of equity capital of the firm?

4. The firm's beta was estimated at 1.1. Treasury bills were yielding 4% and the expected rate of return on the market index was estimated to be 12%. Using various combinations of debt and equity, under the assumption that the costs of each component stays constant, show the effect of increasing leverage on the weighted average cost of capital of the firm. Is there a particular capital structure that maximizes the value of the firm? Explain.

5. How would the key profitability ratios of the firm be affected if the firm were to raise all of the capital by issuing 5-year notes?

6. If you were Andrew Lamb, what would you recommend to the board and why?

7. What are some issues to be concerned about when increasing leverage?

8. Is it fair to assume that if profitability is positively effected in the short run, due to the higher debt ratio, the stock price would increase? Explain.

9. Using suitable diagrams and the data in the case explain how Andrew Lamb could enlighten the board members about Modigliani and Miller's Propositions I and II (with corporate taxes).

20

Bankruptcy and Reorganization

Is It Worth More Dead or Alive?

Robert Falkner, President of Falkner Investments Inc., was faced with a major decision. One of the firms that his company had invested in, Spandex Corporation, was under severe financial distress. It had therefore sent out a proposal for reorganization, which if approved by a majority of the creditors, would lead to a 'pre-pack', in the hope that the company could restructure itself and be salvaged. Being rather unfamiliar with the various regulations and nuances associated with corporate bankruptcy, Robert summoned his Chief Financial Officer, Matt Rodgers. "I am really stumped on this one, Matt," said Robert, pointing to the proposal lying on his desk. "First bankruptcy case that I have encountered in my fifteen years of investing. I'd like you to take a look at the numbers and the proposal and make a recommendation whether I should vote for or against the reorganization plan!"

The Spandex Corporation, incorporated in 1985, designed, manufactured, imported, and marketed various menswear, children's sleepwear and underwear, and other apparel products. It sold its products to department and specialty stores, national chains, major discounters, and mass volume retailers throughout the United States. About 9 years earlier, when sales were booming, the company undertook a major business expansion, almost doubling its manufacturing capacity. The expansion was primarily financed by the issuance of senior notes and preferred stock. However, due to significantly low profit margins and declining demand caused by increasing competition and weak economic conditions, the company faced negative earnings and poor liquidity conditions during the past three years.

Initial attempts to cut costs did alleviate the problems a bit, but with the debt servicing costs being fairly high, the company's cash flows declined sharply. With the senior notes coming up for redemption within a year, the company's management was concerned that they would not be able to refinance the debt nor have the liquidity to pay off the creditors in time. They had therefore embarked upon a voluntary reorganization plan by which the debt would be exchanged for common stock, if agreed upon by the majority of creditors. Table 1 shows the latest balance sheet of the company.

Robert Falkner had purchased $5 million worth of Spandex Corporation's senior notes, about nine years ago. The industry outlook was good and the 10.5% yield on the 10-year notes certainly looked enticing. The company had demonstrated a good record of complying with its interest and dividend obligations and analysts were bullish on the performance of Spandex's common stock.

In their letter to the creditors, Spandex Corporation's management had explained that the current situation was in their opinion, temporary, and that if given a chance to reorganize and restructure, they would do their best to steer the company back on the road to profitability. It was their intention to arrive at an agreement with the majority of creditors and then go for a prepackaged bankruptcy. The reorganization plan called for the exchange of 90.5805 shares of new common stock for each $1000 face vale of the senior debt. The management pointed out that if the firm was forced to liquidate, its current assets could probably be sold for about 40% of book value and its fixed assets would bring in about $9 million. However, roughly 20% of the gross proceeds would have to be paid towards administrative fees and other charges.

After reading the letter and going over the financial statements of Spandex, Robert Faulkner, was clearly undecided. On the one hand, it seemed as if the management team was serious and confident about being able to weather this storm and make the company profitable once again. But, on the other hand, Robert was concerned that the problems could get worse and he could end up with nothing. He was hoping that Matt Rodgers, his CFO, would be able to shed some light on this matter and help him decide whether Spandex was worth more dead or alive!

Table 1

Spandex Corporation		
Latest Fiscal Year Balance Sheet ('000s)		
Current Assets	$ 140,000	Accounts Payable	$ 35,000
		Notes Payables	18,000
Net Fixed Assets	20,000	Accrued Wages	1,800
		Federal Taxes Due	1,000
		State & Local Taxes Due	200
		Current Liabilities	56,000
		First Mortgage	10,000
		Second Mortgage	2,000
		10.5% Senior Notes	14,000
		Long-term debt	26,000
		Preferred Stock	3,500
		Common Stock	46,000
		Paid in Capital	8,000
		Retained Earnings	20,500
		Total Equity	78,000
Total Assets	160,000	Total Liabilities and Owners' Equity	160,000

Questions:

1.   What are the various ways in which firms can be financially distressed? What seemed to be the main problem at Spandex Corporation?

2.   What does the "absolute priority rule" mean? Develop a priority list for Spandex that would be followed if it were liquidated.

3.   Why has Spandex's management attempted to get a pre-packaged bankruptcy?

4.   Define the following terms within the context of this case:

   a.   Workout;
   b.   Reschedule/restructure;
   c.   Extension;
   d.   Composition;
   e.   "Cram down;"
   f.   Automatic stay.

5.   How does insolvency differ from bankruptcy? Which one applies to Spandex and why?

6.   If you were Matt Rodgers, how would you explain the differences between bankruptcy reorganization and bankruptcy liquidation to Robert Falkner?

7.   Should Robert vote in favor of or against the voluntary reorganization? Explain why by performing the necessary calculations.

21

Dividend Policy

Is It Much Ado About Nothing?

It was the end of the fourth quarter. The financial statements had been prepared and circulated to the directors of The New Wave Corporation (see Tables 1 and 2). The firm's revenues had surpassed the previous quarter's revenues by over 20% and the annual sales were approximately 15% higher as well. More importantly, the net income figures for the year were up by more than 25%. The restructuring and cost cutting seemed to have paid off. Needless to say, the mood at the corporate headquarters in Dallas, Texas was upbeat and full of cheer. This year's performance ended a long streak of "down" years and mounting losses. The big question weighing heavily on everyone's minds was "When will they ever pay a dividend?" That exactly was to be the main topic of discussion at that day's meeting of the board of directors.

Edwin Rosewood, a retired biochemist, founded The New Wave Corporation, approximately 12 years ago in his hometown of

Skokie, Illinois. With $500,000 of his own money and the rest borrowed from a local banker, Edwin started manufacturing various patented lotions, hair color dyes, and facial creams in his small facility. Initially, business was slow and it took the company almost 3 years before it made its first profit. Soon thereafter, having struck some major deals with overseas clients, New Wave began to do well. Sales started to climb and the company shifted its headquarters to Dallas, Texas, after issuing 1,000,000 shares in an initial public offering. Although the company made good profits during the next 4 years, the board of directors had decided to retain all of the earnings and reinvest them into the business. They did so for a couple of years and then owing to a downturn in the economy and excessive expenses, the company ended a number of years in the red. Luckily, the company had not accumulated excessive amounts of debt and was able to withstand the difficult times quite well. During this down period the stock price went from a high of $25 to a low of $2. It was currently trading at $8 per share with a P/E ratio of 8.33.

As the directors gathered together for the meeting, Ed, the President and Chief Executive officer, knew that this was going to be an interesting meeting given the significantly different backgrounds, personalities, and beliefs of each director. No sooner had he completed his introductory remarks and popped the question regarding the dividend policy issue than....Joe Smolinski raised his hand, "Why fix it, if it ain't broke?" he said in his usual flippant style. I think we should continue retaining all our earnings and use the money for future investments. I think it would be financially imprudent for us to pay dividends when we know that we are going to have to raise $1,000,000 for that expansion project we had approved last month. Why pay the floatation costs? Besides, don't stock prices almost always drop after the payment of dividends?"

Edwin knew that he had opened a can of worms. He could just feel the room begin to erupt. Right enough, up went Jim Baker's long arm. "I think we owe it to our shareholders. They have waited a long time for a dividend and might vote with their feet if we don't pay any dividends. I think we should identify our existing shareholder groups and make a decision based on what the majority prefers," (see Table 3 for shareholding information.)

Janet Long, who had a degree in finance from one of the top schools in the country, and had read about Modigliani and Miller's (M&Ms) "dividend irrelevancy" proposition, couldn't hold back any longer. "Gentlemen," she said. "Isn't this much ado about nothing? I think we are wasting our time arguing about whether or not dividends should be paid and if so, how much. I think it really doesn't matter one way or the other as far as stock prices are concerned. Those shareholders who don't like our dividend policy can create "homemade dividends for all I care. I think we need to move on to more important issues, like where we are going to have our next annual general meeting." Surprisingly, nobody smiled. "Folks, I'm just kidding." she said. "I think we should use the 'residual dividend' approach," said Bob McKay. "That way we can keep our shareholders happy and maintain our target capital structure. I tend to agree with Jim. The shareholders are expecting some kind of dividend and if we don't deliver, we could be hurting the stock price. But we have to be able to continue supporting whatever dividend payout ratio we go with or else the negative information backlash could come back to haunt us."

Edwin, who had kept silent through much of this discussion finally broke in, "I have somewhat of a different suggestion," he said. "Why don't we figure out how much we can afford to pay out based on our immediate investment needs and target capital structure and then repurchase stock at the prevailing market price with what's left over. That way there would be less of a tax disadvantage to our rich clients and it wouldn't be bad for our EPS either. What do you all think?" There was a long pause in the room. The directors had not considered this option and were stumped. "Let's all go back and rework the numbers," said Edwin, eager to break the silence. "We'll sort this out by tomorrow. Now, let's move on to the next item on the agenda."

Table 1

The New Wave Corporation
Analysis of shareholder groups

Investor group	Number of shareholders	Shares held	% of total shares held
Pension funds	20	240,000	24%
Insurance companies	10	60,000	6%
Mutual Funds	50	130,000	13%
Individuals	10,000	570,000	57%
	10,080	1,000,000	100%

Table 2

The New Wave Corporation
Income Statement

	Current Year
Sales	$ 20,000,000
Cost of goods sold	14,400,000
Gross profit	5,600,000
Selling and administration expenses	3,365,000
Depreciation	300,000
Earnings before interest and taxes	1,935,000
Interest expense	335,000
Earnings before taxes	1,600,000
Taxes	640,000
Net Income	960,000

Table 3

The New Wave Corporation
Balance Sheet

Cash	$ 250,000	Accounts Payable	$ 300,000
Accounts Receivable	$ 450,000	Accruals	$ 250,000
Inventory	$ 675,000	Deferred taxes	$ 100,000
Total Current Assets	$ 1,375,000	**Total Current Liabilities**	$ 650,000
		Long-term debt	$ 3,350,000
Net Fixed Assets	$ 8,000,000	**Total Liabilities**	$ 4,000,000
		Common stock:	
Intangibles	$ 625,000	Par Value	$ 2,000,000
		Paid In Capital	$ 3,000,000
		Retained Earnings	$ 1,000,000
		Shareholders' Equity	$ 6,000,000
Total Assets	$ 10,000,000	**Total Liabilities& Shareholders' Equity**	$10,000,000

Questions:

1. Comment on Joe Smolinski's suggestion of not paying any dividend. What are the pros and cons of such a policy?

2. Critically evaluate Jim Baker's argument that shareholders are expecting a dividend and if not paid one the share price will suffer. Does he have a point? Please explain.

3. What did Janet Long mean when she said, "those shareholders who don't like our dividend policy can create "homemade dividends"? How can one make homemade dividends? Assume you are a shareholder who owns $1000 shares and are expecting the company to pay at least $0.25 per share. If the company decides to retain all its earnings, how can you create homemade dividends?

4. What does the composition of shareholder groups within a corporation have to do with dividend policy? Based on the majority shareholding groups and their relative proportions of ownership in the company, what sort of dividend policy should New Wave adopt?

5. How does a residual dividend policy work? Based on a residual dividend policy how much dividend per share can the company afford to pay? Assume that the company's bonds are trading at par value.

6. What are some of the drawbacks of following a strict residual dividend policy? What do firms typically do in practice?

7. Critically evaluate Ed's suggestion of following a residual dividend policy accompanied by a repurchase of stock at $8 per share. What are the pros and cons of using a stock repurchase option instead of a cash dividend to distribute returns to shareholders.

8. Comment on the dividend policy debate at the New Wave Corporation. In your opinion should they pay dividends at all? Why or why not? If they decide to pay dividends, what kind of dividend policy should they adopt? Please explain.

22

Working Capital Management

Timing Is Everything!

"We have done it again," said Tom Brampton, the president and chief executive officer of Advanced Outboard Motors, to his group of senior managers at their January meeting. "Our sales for this past year are up over 8% compared to the previous year, but our net profit margin and earnings per share are down! The shareholders are understandably upset and are demanding answers. It won't be long before the analysts change their recommendations. We better come up with some explanations and strategies to rectify the problem."

Advanced Outboard Motors, headquartered in Tampa, Florida, had manufacturing facilities in Blaine, Washington and Gary, Indiana. It specialized in the manufacture of outboard motors of various capacities, for small to medium sized boats. The average selling price of its motors was $4000 and the cost of production was $2800 per unit.

The company had been in business for over 10 years and was well respected in the industry.

In particular, analysts had rated its after-sales service, consumer relations, and treatment of employees pretty high in comparison with its competitors. The company's stock (AOMI), which traded in the over the counter market, had appreciated significantly up until the first quarter of the year. After that, however, the company had reported a drop in EPS for three quarters in a row causing the stock price to go down and the shareholders to make frantic calls to the consumer relations office.

"I think I know what the problem is, Tom," said Andy Burgess, the vice-president of finance. "I have taken a look at our financial statements (see Tables 1 and 2) and inventory figures for last year (see Table 3). While most of the expenses seem to be reasonable, I strongly believe that the policy of level monthly production, which was implemented at the start of the year, is the main culprit. Ours is a seasonal business with the peak season being during the months of May-August. Yet, we seem to be maintaining a level production rate of 600 motors per month. As a result, our inventory builds up significantly during the lean months and sits there tying up our capital. With interest rates as high as they have been on our short- term borrowing (prime rate plus 3%, i.e. 9% plus 3%), the interest charges have been killing our profits.

As you can see in this cash budget that I have prepared (Table 4), our short-term debt varied between $2.09 million and $7.09 million during the first six months of the year. We ended the year with no short-term debt, but ended up paying almost $290,000 in interest expenses for the year. That's money that was spent primarily to finance inventory, which I might add, sat around for a few months. I recommend that we drop the level production policy and align our monthly production output with the forecasted sales for the month. I haven't worked out all the numbers yet, but I am quite sure that we will be able to boost our earnings quite a bit by making that change."

"Wait a minute," said Gary Cooper, the production manager, from the other side of the room. "Have you considered the effect of that change on our workforce and employee morale? We will have to lay off people during lean times and scramble to hire more workers during peak production periods. That will have a negative effect on our operating efficiency and will result in some additional costs for training and orientation. My staff and I are in contact with these folks on a daily basis. I would hate to have to tell some of these "nice" folks that they were being laid off for a few months, especially when our annual sales have been going up. There's got to be a better way!"

"Gentlemen," said Tom Brampton, sensing that that the arguments were getting rather heated. "Let's not jump to any conclusions here. I think you both have expressed valid points. On the one hand, we can't lose sight of the fact that we value our employees and must continue caring for them. Yet on the other, we cannot let our earnings and stock price keep on dropping, especially considering the fact that our sales have been going up on a consistent basis. As you all know, the market can be merciless, once the analysts' change their tone. Andy, why don't you do the necessary number crunching and present the results at our next meeting. Let's analyze all aspects of our working capital management policies and try and come up with the best possible alternative. I think this experience clearly proves that in our business, as in most businesses, timing is everything!"

Table 1

Advanced Outboard Motors	
Income Statement	
Sales	$ 28,800,000
Cost of Goods Sold	20,160,000
Gross Profit	**8,640,000**
Overheads	4,809,600
Depreciation	1,000,000
Earnings before Interest & taxes	**2,830,400**
Interest	1,500,000
Earnings before taxes	**1,330,400**
Taxes	466,400
Net Income	**864,000**

Table 2

Advanced Outboard Motors			
Balance Sheet			
Cash	918,280	Accounts Payable	1,680,000
Accounts Receivable	129,600	Short-term Debt	-
Inventory	4,060,000		
Total Current Assets	**5,107,880**	**Total Current Liabilities**	**1,680,000**
		LTD	10,820,000
Net Fixed Assets	13,152,120	*Total Liabilities*	*12,500,000*
		Equity (1 million shares)	5,760,000
		Liabilities & Owner's	
Total Assets	**18,260,000**	**Equity**	**18,260,000**

Table 3

Monthly Sales (units), Production Output (units), and Inventory Values

	Beg. Inv.	Production	Sales	End. Inv	Inventory Value @$2800 each
January	1450	600	0	2050	$ 5,740,000
February	2050	600	0	2650	7,420,000
March	2650	600	200	3050	8,540,000
April	3050	600	600	3050	8,540,000
May	3050	600	1200	2450	6,860,000
June	2450	600	1500	1550	4,340,000
July	1550	600	1640	510	1,428,000
August	510	600	1000	110	308,000
Sept	110	600	700	10	28,000
Oct	10	600	200	410	1,148,000
Nov	410	600	106	904	2,531,200
Dec	904	600	54	1450	4,060,000

Table 4

Cash Budget (with borrowing/repayment of loans)

	Rate	Dec (Last Year)	Jan	Feb	Mar	Apr	May
Unit Sales		50	0	0	200	600	1200
Revenues	$4,000	200,000	-	-	800,000	2,400,000	4,800,000
Cash Receipts							
Cash Sales	40%	78,400	-	-	313,600	940,800	1,881,600
Collections (Prior Month's sales)	60%		120,000	-	-	480,000	1,440,000
Total Cash Receipts			120,000	-	313,600	1,420,800	3,321,600
Production (units)			600	600	600	600	600
Production Costs	2800		1,680,000	1,680,000	1,680,000	1,680,000	1,680,000
Cash Payments							
Production costs		1,680,000	1,680,000	1,680,000	1,680,000	1,680,000	1,680,000
Overhead		400,800	400,800	400,800	400,800	400,800	400,800
Interest			125,000	125,000	125,000	125,000	125,000
Taxes					116,600		
Total Cash Payments			2,205,800	2,205,800	2,322,400	2,205,800	2,205,800
Net Cash Flow			(2,085,800)	(2,205,800)	(2,008,800)	(785,000)	1,115,800
Beginning Cash Bal.			200,000	200,000	200,000	200,000	200,000
Cumulative Cash Bal.			(1,885,800)	(2,005,800)	(1,808,800)	(585,000)	1,315,800
Monthly Loan/repayment			2,085,800	2,205,800	2,008,800	785,000	(1,115,800)
Cumulative Loan			2,085,800	4,291,600	6,300,400	7,085,400	5,969,600
Ending Cash*			200,000	200,000	200,000	200,000	200,000
Cumulative Loan			2085800	4291600	6300400	7085400	5969600
Interest Expense	1%		20858	42916	63004	70854	59696

Table 4 (Continued)

Cash Budget (with borrowing/repayment of loans)

	Rate	Jun	July	Aug	Sep	Oct	Nov	Dec
Unit Sales		1500	1640	1000	700	200	106	54
Revenues	$ 4,000	6,000,000	$6,560,000	$4,000,000	$ 2,800,000	800,000	424,000	216,000
Cash Receipts								
Cash Sales	40%	2,352,000	2,571,520	1,568,000	1,097,600	313,600	166,208	84,672
Collections (Prior Month's sales)	60%	2,880,000	3,600,000	3,936,000	2,400,000	1,680,000	480,000	254,400
Total Cash Receipts		5,232,000	6,171,520	5,504,000	3,497,600	1,993,600	646,208	339,072
Production (units)		600	600	600	600	600	600	600
Production Costs	2800	1,680,000	1,680,000	1,680,000	1,680,000	1,680,000	1,680,000	1,680,000
Cash Payments								
Production costs		1,680,000	1,680,000	1,680,000	1,680,000	1,680,000	1,680,000	1,680,000
Overhead		400,800	400,800	400,800	400,800	400,800	400,800	400,800
Interest		125,000	125,000	125,000	125,000	125,000	125,000	125,000
Taxes		116,600			116,600			116,600
Total Cash Payments		2,322,400	2,205,800	2,205,800	2,322,400	2,205,800	2,205,800	2,322,400
Net Cash Flow		2,909,600	3,965,720	3,298,200	1,175,200	(212,200)	(1,559,592)	(1,983,328)
Beginning Cash Bal.		200,000	200,000	200,000	3,498,200	4,673,400	4,461,200	2,901,608
Cumulative Cash Bal.		3,109,600	4,165,720	3,498,200	4,673,400	4,461,200	2,901,608	918,280
Monthly Loan/repayment		(2,909,600)	(3,060,000)	-	-	-	-	-
Cumulative Loan		3,060,000	-	-	-	-	-	-
Ending Cash		200,000	200,000	3,498,200	4,673,400	4,461,200	2,901,608	918,280
Cumulative Loan		3060000	0	0	0	0	0	0
Interest Expense	1%	30600	0	0	0	0	0	0

Questions:

1. Comment on Advanced Outboard Motors' absolute and relative liquidity positions.

2. Examine the company's monthly inventory turnover ratio. What does it indicate?

3. How long are the firm's operating and cash cycles? Using a suitable diagram show the breakdown of the firm's operating cycle into its relevant components. What do your findings indicate?

4. How much higher would the firm's earnings per share have been if it had followed a policy of aligning the production output with the number of units sold each month?

5. Calculate the monthly net working capital figures for the company. Comment on your findings.

6. Is the firm following an aggressive or a conservative financing policy for funding its working capital? Explain.

7. Is Andy correct in stating that the main culprit is the firm's production policy? Besides changing the production levels per month, are there any other things that the firm can realistically do to boost earnings per share?

8. Using Dupont analysis, comment on the firm's profit situation.

9. Do you agree with the production manager's comment that that "there's got to be a better way?" Please explain.

23

Cash Budgeting

Getting Our Act Together

"I know that I have got to do better short-term planning" said Mark Wahl to his wife, Elizabeth, as he put down the telephone. "John, our bank manager, is getting rather anxious about our recurrent cash shortfalls." He just cautioned me that the bank might have to raise their rates on us if another over draft occurs. That can really hurt us and our suppliers are not happy either.

Mark Wahl, the owner of Best Electronics, had operated a fairly successful retail outlet for electronic goods over the past five years. The firm had two locations and over the past year had expanded quite significantly into the wholesale supply of electronic components as well. Revenues were up by 20% over the past year and net profits had increased by about 10%. However, ever since the company got involved in the wholesale supply business their cash account had fluctuated significantly during the year resulting in 4 overdraft notices from the bank. About six months ago the company had set up an overdraft protection reserve account (First Reserve Account) with a limit of $50,000 with their bank, but even that amount had been exceeded a couple of times.

"Why don't you ask your MBA intern, Joe Ferguson, to prepare a monthly cash budget for the firm for the next twelve months?" asked Elizabeth. "I think he has spent too much time analyzing our "just-in-time" inventory system and should be able to put his excellent financial skills to better use."

"That's the best suggestion you have made in a long time," joked Mark with a chuckle. "I will meet with him first thing tomorrow morning. I think we had better get our act together before our suppliers and creditors start locking us out!"

At their meeting, Mark presented Joe with sales projections for the next thirteen months as shown in Table 1. The financial staff of Best Electronics had done a fairly good job of tracking its sales and purchases over time and had projected monthly sales for the next year. These projections were based on historical trends and feedback from the sales staff. Retail sales were mostly made on a cash basis but wholesale orders carried credit terms ranging from 30 to 60 days. As a result, typically, 40% of their monthly sales were collected in the same month, with another 30% in the following month, and the rest in 60 days. On average, 2% of each month's credit sales were deemed to be bad debts. Sales in November and December of the previous year amounted to $850,000 and $875,000 respectively.

Purchases typically amounted to 80% of the following month's projected sales and were paid for in the month following delivery. The firm employed a staff of about 30 employees and paid out salaries of $50,000 per month. Debt payments amounted to $3,000 per month, and other expenses were estimated to be $6,000 per month. The depreciation on fixed assets was calculated to be $8,000 for the coming year. The firm had already approved a request to purchase new computer equipment for $20,000, the payment for which would have to be made in June of the following year. The accountants estimated that taxes for the coming year would amount to $560,000 and would be paid on a quarterly basis.

Table 1

Estimated monthly sales for next 13 months

January	$350,000	July	$600,000
February	$300,000	August	$625,000
March	$250,000	September	$700,000
April	$400,000	October	$725,000
May	$500,000	November	$800,000
June	$525,000	December	$900,000
		January	$400,000

Questions:

1. Even though sales have been increasing, why is Best Electronics in such a cash flow crunch?

2. What does the firm need to do as soon as possible?

3. Prepare the collections worksheet. Which month has the greatest amount of cash inflows?

4. Prepare the disbursements worksheet. Which months seem to be hit by the highest amount of cash outflows? Why? Can this trend be changed?

5. How should the depreciation expense be treated in the cash budget?

6. Which months seem to be particularly vulnerable to cash deficits? Which months have the greatest surpluses?

7. If the cash balance outstanding is -$2,000, help Joe develop a cash budget for Best Electronics for the next twelve months. How can Mark use the cash budget to minimize cash shortages and plan for the future?

8. Given that the monthly sales figures have been fluctuating so much what should Joe do while preparing the cash budget? Can he take the sales figures provided by the finance department at face value? If so why? If not why? What other options does he have?

9. How can a minimum cash balance be built in? How much of a minimum cash balance seems warranted? What can the company do with the excess cash that is generated in some months?

10. Rework the budget by using your suggested minimum cash balance and assume that short-term loans carry an interest rate of 8% per year.

24

Cash Budgeting

The Elusive Cash Balance

"What do you mean we've used up all our cash and lines of credit? I don't get it! I thought we had a healthy financial position as per last year's financial statements. How could this have happened, Carl?" said Robert McGovern to his chief accountant. "If our suppliers find out, we could be in a compromising position. I can't let that happen. Why don't you prepare a detailed report including a cash budget for the next year and give it to by 10 AM tomorrow. Build in a minimum cash balance that is at least 25% higher than our last year's ending cash balance, but make sure that it's not more than 50% higher in any period.

Robert McGovern, the owner of McGovern Distributing Inc., had inherited the family business 5 year's ago, when his father, Bradley, suddenly passed away. Under Brad's leadership, the firm had grown slowly but steadily. Brad had always maintained strong ties with local businesses, suppliers, and customers. As Carl began looking at the financial statements (see Tables 1 and 2), he couldn't help recalling how Bradley had managed to always keep the firm's liquidity position strong by being conservative and planning for the future. He did not take undue risk and only accepted products of the highest quality for distribution. Bills were always paid on time and credit terms were only extended to those customers and retailers who were well known to Bradley (most were!).

Robert, on the other hand, had always criticized his father's conservative business policies. As soon as he took over, he unleashed a whole host of liberal terms and policies. He significantly expanded the list of products offered for distribution to retailers, extended much longer credit periods to clients, and took on a lot of additional bank loans to finance his expansions. The list of product offerings grew from 300 to 650 and the number of suppliers more than tripled. Although revenues increased during the five-year period, the volatility increased as well. More importantly, the cash balance had been very unstable and had significantly decreased over time, indicating a problem in cash management.

As Carl crunched out the numbers, he realized that in order to prepare a detailed cash budget and financial report he would need to figure out the average receivables period, the average payables period, and a periodic sales forecast.   He figured that he would make the assumption that sales would increase at the last year's rate of 25%. After consulting the sales manager, Carl developed a breakdown of monthly sales for the last quarter of 2001 and for the forthcoming year (see Table 3). Table 4 presents the collection schedule that Carl assumed the firm would follow in the coming year. All other expenses and charges would be assumed to vary proportionately with sales or held constant. Carl was aware that the firm would be acquiring a new delivery truck for $40,000 in May of the coming year and figured that he better include it in the cash budget. All operating expenses were uniformly distributed over the year. Debt payments were made monthly while taxes were paid in March, June, September, and December of each year.   The firm had a policy of ordering goods one month in advance of forecasted sales and would pay for them within around 90 days.

As he glanced at his watch, Carl realized that he better get some assistance or he would have to face an irate boss in the morning. He picked up the telephone and called for Lisa, his recently hired assistant, to come to his rescue in solving this problem of the "elusive cash balance."

Table 1

McGovern Distributing Inc.

Income Statements

	2001	2000	1999
Sales	$6,100,000	$4,880,000	$4,000,000
Cost of Goods Sold	4,880,000	3,904,000	3,200,000
Gross Profit	1,220,000	976,000	800,000
Salaries	610,000	488,000	400,000
Utilities	16,000	14,000	12,000
Other Expenses	61,000	48,800	40,000
Depreciation	15,000	15,000	15,000
Earnings Before Interest and Taxes	518,000	410,200	333,000
Interest Paid	73,455	61,000	46,000
Earnings Before Taxes	444,545	349,200	287,000
Taxes	155,591	122,220	100,450
Net Income	288,954	226,980	186,550

Table 2

McGovern Distributing Inc.

Balance Sheets

	2001	2000	1999
Assets			
Cash and Cash Equivalents	$57,154	$48,800	160,000
Accounts Receivable	700,000	600,000	450,000
Inventory	$1,000,000	$619,847	300,000
Total Current Assets	1,757,154	1,268,647	910,000
Gross Fixed Assets	750,000	750,000	750,000
Accumulated Depreciation	145,000	130,000	115,000
Net Plant & Equipment	605,000	620,000	635,000
Total Assets	2,362,154	1,888,647	1,545,000
Liabilities and Owner's Equity			
Accounts Payable	$350,000	$300,000	$200,000
Bank Loan @ 10% per year	574,553	450,000	300,000
Other Current Liabilities	80,000	70,000	50,000
Total Current Liabilities	$1,004,553	$820,000	$550,000
Long-term Debt	200,000	200,000	200,000
Total Liabilities			
Owner's Capital	$355,117	$355,117	$508,450
Retained Earnings	802,484	513,530	286,550
Total Liabilities and Owner's Equity	2,362,154	1,888,647	1,545,000

Table 3

Month	Actual Sales	Expected Sales
Oct-01	400,000	------
Nov-01	450,000	------
Dec-01	600,000	------
Jan-02	------	300,000
Feb-02	------	400,000
Mar-02	------	500,000
Apr-02	------	500,000
May-02	------	500,000
Jun-02	------	600,000
Jul-02	------	700,000
Aug-02	------	600,000
Sep-02	------	700,000
Oct-02	------	800,000
Nov-02	------	825,000
Dec-02	------	1,200,000
Jan-03	------	350,000
Feb-03	------	450,000

Table 4

Collection Schedule	
<30 days	20%
31-60 days	40%
61-90 days	40%
Bad Debts	3%

Questions:

1. What seems to be the major problem with McGovern Distributing Inc.? Why has this problem occurred?

2. Based on the prior years' financial statements, what conclusion do you think Carl would be justified in reaching? What calculations should he make to analyze the cash position of the company? Substantiate your answer by making the necessary calculations.

3. Should Carl prepare a quarterly or a monthly cash budget for McGovern Distributing Inc.? Explain why.

4. Prepare a suitable cash budget for McGovern Distributing Inc. Build in a minimum cash balance and a maximum cash balance as requested by Robert. Assume that the cash position at the start of the budgeting period is zero.

5. Based on your calculations, which months seem to be the most vulnerable to cash deficits and which ones have the greatest surplus funds?

6. If borrowed funds cost 10% per year and excess funds can be invested at 6% per year, prepare an annual financial plan for McGovern Distributing Inc.

7. How might the firm avoid cash shortages in the future? Please explain.

8. Based on the data provided calculate and comment on the absolute liquidity of McGovern Distributing Inc.

25

A Switch in Time Saves Nine

Allan sat at his office desk pondering over what was discussed at his last meeting with the Treasurer, Jill Haas. The working capital of their firm, Modern Farm Equipment Incorporated, had increased at an alarming rate over the past couple of years making the directors and top managers very concerned. Despite the implementation of a 'just in time' inventory system and more efficient cash management methods, the working capital continued to rise. This time, however, it was the accounts receivables that needed attention. Jill received a memo from the board asking her to review and rectify the credit management problem as soon as possible. One of the sentences in the memo read "...we simply cannot continue to carry our customers as long as we have been." Jill had therefore called on her assistant, Allan Donald, and briefed him of the situation.

Modern Farm Equipment Inc. had been in business since 1945, producing small and medium sized tractors, tillers, and other farm equipment. Its customer base included various local and regional hardware stores, farm equipment stores, and repair shops. Most of the clients were strapped for cash and were accustomed to fairly flexible credit terms. The firm had been hard pressed to offer terms of net 60 to its clients, primarily to counter competition from national suppliers and to maintain good customer relationships.

Sales had steadily increased over the years but over the past year, higher interest rates and a weakening economy had caused a slump in the agricultural sector leading to a drop in sales of farm equipment. Moreover, the number of farmers filing for bankruptcy had been increasing at an alarming rate.

As Jill and Allan reviewed the accounting statements (see Tables 1 and 2) and the aging schedule of receivables, they realized that despite the fairly liberal credit terms of net 60, on average, 40% of the credit sales were being collected 10 days late. The company had not had a policy of charging interest or late fees so as to avoid losing customers. They also noticed that over the past year the number of bad debts had gone up from 1% of sales to its current level of 2% of sales.

Jill told Allan that the directors expected to see a proposal that would be realistic and effective. "On the one hand, we have to be careful about not turning customers away," said Jill. "But on the other hand, we simply cannot afford to continue the current policy of allowing customers to pay late. Some credit will have to be given, but collections have to be tightened up. I guess the time has come for us to 'switch or suffer.'"

About six months earlier, Jill Haas recruited Allan Donald, a certified financial manager, to assist her in managing the company's working capital. Initially, it was the management of cash and inventory that needed modification. After much debate and discussion, a more conservative policy of cash management was implemented, followed by a successful integration of a just-in-time inventory management system. The quarterly statements showed that the modifications had worked. Jill and Allan were aware that the company's collection policy was rather liberal. However, given the economic conditions and sensitivity of the issue, they had refrained from suggesting any changes.

As Allan pondered about what changes in collections policy he should recommend he realized that he would have to get some more data. He called up the folks in marketing and inquired about what effect a tighter collection policy would have. Upon being asked to be more specific, he told them that he was considering two alternatives:

1) 2/10 net 30, and
2) 2/10 net 60.

He was told that under the first alternative, sales would probably decrease by about 10%. The sales people had built up a very good relationship with their customers and were confident that, despite the tighter credit terms, they could retain most of the accounts provided there was some incentive for paying early. Moreover, they informed Allan that most retailers could avail of commercial loans from banks at an average rate of interest of 16% per year. If the second alternative were implemented, the accounts receivables figure would be reduced without any loss of sales. Obviously, the sales people preferred the second approach. Allan estimated that under the new terms approximately 50 percent of sales would be collected within 10 days. Of the remaining 50% of sales, roughly 60% would be collected within the credit period and the remaining 40% would be approximately 10 days late, as usual. Allan figured that he had better prepare pro forma statements showing the impact that these policies would have on the company's bottom line and on the accounts receivable balance, before recommending any harsh penalties and so on.

Table 1

Modern Farm Equipment Incorporated
Latest Fiscal Year's Income Statement ('000s)

Sales	30000
Cost of Goods Sold	19500
Gross Profit	10500
Op. Expenses	4800
Earnings Before Interest and Taxes	5700
Interest expenses (10% per year)	1300
Earnings Before Taxes	4400
Income taxes	2280
Net Income	2120

Table 2

Modern Farm Equipment Incorporated
Latest Fiscal Year's Balance Sheet ('000s)

Cash	2000	Accounts Payable	3200
Accounts Receivable	5260	Notes Payable	5000
Inventory	6000	Total Current Liabilities	8200
Total Current Assets	13260	Long-Term Debt	8000
Fixed Assets	20000	Stockholders' Equity	17060
Total Assets	33260	Total Liabilities and equity	33260

Questions:

1.   What are the elements of a good credit policy? Evaluate Modern Farm Equipment's credit policy.

2.   Why is the increase in accounts receivables of concern to the board of directors? Are they justified in their demand for a tighter credit policy? Why?

3.   What is the amount of annual expense to the firm as a result of the delay in collections? What other risks do such delays entail?

4.   Calculate the cost of foregoing the 2% cash discount offered under the 2/10, net 30 and 2/10 net 60 terms respectively. Given that most retailers could take short term loans from banks at the rate of 16% or less, evaluate the attractiveness of each policy.

5.   What are some other ways in which the company could speed up collections and reduce the receivables?

6.   Why has this slow build up in accounts receivables occurred? Could it have been avoided? How? Please explain.

7.   Develop the pro forma financial statements for the company under the two credit policy alternatives, i.e. 2/10, net 60; and 2/10 net 30 using the assumptions given. What would be the impact on the firm's return on sales, return on investment, and return on equity?

8.   Which policy should Allan recommend to the board? Why?

26

International Capital Budgeting

Will it Be Worthwhile to Venture?

"We better get started on this report," said Mike to his assistant, Brad, as he straightened his seatback and fired up his laptop computer. "I'm sure Ron will expect a detailed analysis first thing, Monday morning." Michael Cooper, the Vice President for International Business Development at Murray Technologies and his assistant, Bradley Johnson were returning back to the United States from their 7-day trip to New Delhi, India.

Ron Howard, the President and Chief Executive Officer of Murray Technologies had been contacted by Shah Electronics from India with a proposal of starting a joint venture for the production of circuit boards. Currently, Murray Technologies was exporting 50,000 circuit boards a year to Indian importers at a per unit price of $50 including shipping and insurance. The company had managed to obtain an import agreement from the Indian government for a 10-year period, which was due to expire within one year. The pre-tax profit on the exported circuit boards was $15 per unit (see Table 1 for cost breakdown) and unit sales were expected to increase at the rate of 4% per year based on the projected increase in the gross domestic product in India.

Table 1

Cost Breakdown of Circuit Board (Exported)

Components.......................$20
Labor............................. 10
Freight and Insurance...............5
Total Cost per unit   35

Based on the discussions held with the Indian counterparts, Mike estimated that the cost of establishing the manufacturing facility in India would be around $2,800,000 at the prevailing exchange rate of $1 = 50 Rupees. The Indian partner had agreed to invest 50% of the initial outlay. In addition to fixed assets, Mike estimated that $600,000 worth of working capital would be needed for start-up.

Under the tentative terms of the joint venture, Shah Electronics would manage the day-to-day operations of the business with overall supervision being the responsibility of an American chief engineer. Murray Technologies would turn over the operation to Shah Electronics after 7 years, in exchange for full reimbursement of the working capital and a purchase price amounting to 130% of the net book value of the fixed assets at that time. With the help of Bharat Shah, the managing director of Shah Electronics, Mike had managed to get the Indian government to reach a tentative agreement whereby at the end of each year, Murray's share of net cash flows from the joint venture could be remitted to the USA at the prevailing exchange rate.

Mike had checked with the tax authorities in India and found out that the fixed assets could be depreciated on a straight- line basis over 10 years. The corporate tax rate in India was 40% as in the US. After meeting with various suppliers and checking quality control standards, Mike had worked out the details regarding the revised cost structure of the circuit boards (see Table 2). The circuit boards manufactured in India would be made of a combination of domestic and US components. Mike figured that the net cost of the components imported from the USA (manufactured by Murray Technologies) would be $5 per unit and would be supplied to the joint venture at the rate of $8 per unit. Mike knew that by producing the circuit boards in India, there would be significant labor cost advantages.

Table 2

Cost Breakdown of Circuit Boards manufactured in India

Indigenous Components.....................................$12
Imported Components (supplied by Murray)........... 8
Labor cost per unit 5
Total cost per unit   25

As Brad and Mike began working out the cash flow details, Mike asked Brad, "Do you think it would be better for us to raise the money in India at the rate of 15% per year or borrow the dollars in the US at the rate of 10% and remit the funds to India after conversion at the prevailing exchange rate?" Brad, who had earned an MBA in International Finance, said, "I don't think it really matters, Mike. Based on the principle of covered interest arbitrage, there should be no real advantage one way or another. That's assuming we can raise the money without significantly different transactions costs or other impediments in either country." "I knew that," said Mike. "I was just checking to see if you were still awake." Somehow Brad wasn't convinced.

Mike knew that the required rate of return on projects of this nature was typically 15% in the USA. However, he realized that the nominal risk-free rate in India was 9% compared to 4% in the USA, while the inflation rate was 5% in India and only 2% in the USA. Moreover, it was a policy at Murray Technologies to estimate future foreign exchange rates on the basis of projected inflation rates. Accordingly, Mike had collected inflation rate forecasts for the next seven years for India and the USA (see Table 3)

Table 3

Projected annual inflation rates

	USA	India
Year 1	3%	5%
Year 2	3%	6%
Year 3	4%	8%
Year 4	4%	8%
Year 5	4%	8%
Year 6	4%	8%
Year 7	4%	9%

Mike knew that Ron would demand a comprehensive analysis of all relevant cash flows using both, the "home currency" as well as the "foreign currency" approach. Just as he reached into his briefcase for his financial calculator, there was an announcement on the personal address system, "This is your captain speaking. We are approaching some heavy cloud cover and expect some turbulence, which could be heavy at times. Please return to your seats and fasten your seatbelts until the sign is turned off. Thank you." Mike figured that he better put away the computer and get back to his analysis in the safety and comfort of his office.

Questions:

1. What did Brad mean when he said that, based on covered interest arbitrage, it made no difference whether Murray Technologies raised the capital needed for the joint venture in India or in the USA? Do you agree? Please explain.

2. Based on the differential inflation rate projections, what are the expected end of year exchange rates between the US$ and the Indian rupee for the next seven years?

3. Based on the "home currency" approach what should Mike recommend?

4. Does the decision change if the "foreign currency" approach is used for the analysis? Please explain with the help of adequate calculations.

5. As Mike was inquiring about the tax provisions in India, he was told that there was a high probability that the Indian government would offer a reduced tax rate (20%) to foreign investors who used some indigenous raw materials and employed Indians. If this does happen, how would the analysis be affected?

6. How would Mike's analysis and recommendation change if Murray Technologies intends to use this joint venture as a stepping-stone to maintain a permanent position in India and therefore reinvests its earnings in India?

7. Besides exchange rate fluctuations, what other risk factors would Mike have to take into consideration before making his recommendation?

8. What are the different ways in which Murray's share of the cash flows from the joint venture can be remitted to the USA?

9. Let's assume that Mike was unable to get the Indian government to give him a firm commitment that cash flows earned by Murray Technologies could be freely remitted to the USA. Imports could be paid for immediately but all other cash remittances would be blocked until the end of the fourth year. Funds invested in India could earn a tax-free rate of 4% per year. What effect would this event have on the analysis and recommendation?

27

Hedging with Derivatives

Risky Business

It was a hot, humid afternoon in April and Brandon could feel the pressure mounting. The memo on his desk read, "Please see me immediately!" Brandon knew that, sooner or later, his boss, David Baker, was going to ask him to implement some quick remedies to improve the profit situation. The quarterly financial statements had just been published and for the fourth quarter in a row, The Coppertone Pipe Company had reported a sharp drop in earnings per share despite a consistent increase in revenues. Needless to say, the shareholders were irate and the public relations department had been inundated with calls from concerned shareholders wondering what was going on. In fact, at the annual general meeting held last quarter, the shrinking profits of the firm was the main topic of discussion. It led to the early retirement of the Chief Financial Officer, Russell Smith.

The Coppertone Pipe Company was headquartered in Delaware and had established manufacturing facilities in Illinois, California, Ohio, and Pennsylvania. It specialized in the manufacture of high-grade copper piping of various thickness and circular dimensions. The pipes were used primarily in commercial and residential applications. 70% of its sales were accounted for by exports to the United Kingdom while the rest came from sales to wholesalers in the USA.

Over the past year, copper prices had fluctuated significantly (see Table 1). The firm had been unable to purchase high-grade copper at stable prices, leading to a significant erosion of corporate profits despite surging sales. The orders had been booked at a time when the price of copper was at its lowest level in twelve months ($0.62/lb.). That was the price that had been figured into the cost structure. Unfortunately, due to the stiff competition that characterized the piping industry, Coppertone was unable to shift the price increases on to the wholesalers. To make matters worse, the US$ had strengthened significantly over the prior twelve months resulting in further loss of profits upon conversion of British pounds into dollars. The dollar had gone from $1.55 per pound, twelve months ago, to its current level of $1.43 per pound. Due to the fierce competition in the overseas market, British wholesalers were able to negotiate very favorable terms including ninety days credit and payment in British pounds.

Part of the problem at Coppertone was that the previous CFO, Russ Smith, had not been very familiar with the mechanics of the derivatives market. He had therefore not hedged the company's commodity and exchange rate exposures at all. Upon his retirement, David Baker, was appointed as the CFO. Dave's first move was to recruit Brandon Keenan, a derivatives expert. Brandon had earned an MBA in Finance at a major midwestern university and had worked for five years at the Chicago Mercantile Exchange, prior to joining Coppertone. The company had made him an offer that was too good to resist and Brandon knew that sooner or later the pressure would be on to prove his worth.

Table 1

Historical Spot Prices of High-Grade Copper

Month end		Price (cents/lb.)
May	2001	62.00
June	2001	64.75
July	2001	66.25
August	2001	65.70
September	2001	67.30
October	2001	64.45
November	2001	61.80
December	2001	70.40
January	2002	71.50
February	2002	73.35
March	2002	74.50
April	2002	76.10

In preparation for the meeting with Dave, Brandon gathered information from the purchasing, sales, payables, and receivables departments. The sales department had booked orders for $50 million worth of pipes, 70% of which was from British clients. Brandon estimated that the company would need about 40 million pounds worth of high-grade copper by the end of three months to manufacture the pipes. Copper was being quoted at $0.72 per pound in the spot market and the British pound was quoted at $1.42 per pound. There was a likelihood that copper prices could go down and the dollar could weaken against the British pound, but the reverse could also happen. Brandon knew all too well that the market could go either way. He feared that if copper prices were to appreciate along with the dollar, corporate profits would be significantly affected and he would be out looking for a job. He liked this company and the lavish compensation package he had been offered was definitely worth keeping. "I had better come up with some effective hedging combinations," thought Brandon. "This is no time to take a wait and see approach."

Brandon tapped on his laptop and checked the Internet for the latest quotes on futures contracts trading on the British Pound and on high-grade copper (see Tables 2 –5). After jotting down some numbers and making some quick calculations, Brandon picked up the phone. "Dave," he said with a smile on his face, "About that meeting you wanted to have with me…Can we meet right away?"

Table 2

British Pound Futures – Contract Specifications

Trading unit:	62500 British Pounds
Price Quotation:	US$ per Pound
Trading symbol:	BP
Initial margin:	$1080 per contract
Maintenance margin:	$ 800 per contract

Table 3

British Pound Futures
Settlement prices as of April 2002

MTH/ STRIKE	---- DAILY ---- OPEN	HIGH	LOW	LAST	EST SETT	CHGE	---- PRIOR DAY ---- VOL.	SETT	VOL.	OPEN INT.
JUN02	1.4324	1.4332	1.4296	1.4312	1.4314	-20	1792	1.4334	7901	35237
SEP02	1.4230	1.4256	1.4228	1.4250	1.4234	-20	1	1.4254	31	880
TOTAL							1793		7932	36117

Table 4

Copper Futures – Contract Specifications

Trading unit:	25000 lbs.
Price Quotation:	cents per lb. For example, 75.80 cents per lb.
Trading symbol:	HG
Initial margin:	$1350 per contract
Maintenance margin:	$1000 per contract

Table 5

Copper Futures
Settlement Prices as of April 2002

CONTRACT	EXPIRATION DATE	TODAY'S SETTLE	PREVIOUS SETTLE	VOLUME	DAILY HIGH	DAILY LOW
HG 04 02	4/26/2002	71.5	72.1	64	71.6	71.6
HG 05 02	5/29/2002	71.7	72.3	7,039	72.4	71.2
HG 06 02	6/26/2002	72.05	72.65	58	72.15	71.95
HG 07 02	7/29/2002	72.4	73	1,942	73	71.9
HG 08 02	8/28/2002	72.7	73.3	10	73.1	72.5
HG 09 02	9/26/2002	72.95	73.5	125	73.45	72.75
HG 10 02	10/29/2002	73.2	73.7	3	73.25	73.25
HG 11 02	11/25/2002	73.45	73.95	2	0	0
HG 12 02	12/27/2002	73.7	74.2	234	74.25	73.3

Questions:

1. What is meant by the term 'transactions exposure'? What kind of transactions exposure is The Coppertone Pipe Co. faced with?

2. How much variability has there been in the spot price of high-grade copper over the past twelve months? Is it large enough to warrant the need for hedging? Please explain.

3. What kind of hedging strategy should Brandon recommend for minimizing Coppertone's exposure to volatility in copper prices? Design a suitable hedge and show what would be the result if copper prices went to 78.2 cents per lb. at the end of three months when the company would be ordering the high-grade copper.

4. How should Brandon respond if Dave argues that there is a good chance that copper prices could be coming down?

5. Why is Brandon concerned about the dollar strengthening in value against the British pound?

6. What hedging strategies can Brandon recommend to minimize the impact of exchange rate volatility?

7. Using the data given for British Pound futures contracts design a suitable hedge that would minimize Coppertone's exposure to fluctuations in the exchange rate between the US$ and the British Pound. Explain the results of the hedge if by September 2002, when payment is received from the British wholesalers, the exchange rate goes to $1.33 per British Pound.

8. Dave questions Brandon, "What about forward contracts? Why not use forward contracts instead?" How should Brandon respond?

9. During their meeting, Dave told Brandon that the firm had been forced to use floating-rate loans for expansion due to their low credit rating. Although long-term rates were higher, the firm would have preferred to match the maturity of the debt with the duration of their financing need. Besides, short-term rates had been rising and were expected to continue going up due to rising inflation. The firm currently had borrowed $2 million at a floating rate of prime plus 1% (currently 6.5%). Longer-term, fixed rate debt was available at 9% per year. Dave had heard about interest rate swaps and asked Brandon to explain to him how Coppertone could use a swap to minimize their interest rate risk. How should Brandon respond?

10. Besides an interest rate swap, what other strategies could Brandon recommend to Dave to help minimize the company's exposure to interest rate risk?

28

Valuing Corporate Acquisitions

Made for Each Other

It was late Sunday night and Dan Peterman was getting weary. The big presentation was set for 8 am the next day and Dan kept remembering what Ray Machado, the chairman of the Mergers and Acquisitions (M&A) committee had said to him. "The board members are going to ask several tough questions at the meeting so we better prepare ourselves thoroughly. Make sure that we can substantiate all our numbers and justify all our assumptions."

Dan and Ray were serving on the M&A committee, which had been formed by their CEO, Keith Overby, to "look into" possible candidates for acquisition. The three of them were employed by Innovative Concepts, a fairly large-sized manufacturing firm, headquartered in Minneapolis, Minnesota, which produced unique metal products for household and commercial use.

Formed in 1980, the company had seen better days. At the time of its inception, its industry sector was still in its infancy stage and competition was almost non-existent. As a result the company enjoyed significant growth over the years and was able to recruit excellent personnel, many of who stayed with the company right from the start. The firm had accumulated a significant amount of cash and built up a good credit history.

Over the past couple of years, however, due to fierce competition and a lackluster economy, the firm's scope of expansion had all but dried up, and the managers were hard pressed to search for alternative avenues for growth. The company's stock price had recently dropped to $45 per share. The overwhelming consensus in the boardroom was that the firm should look for suitable acquisition candidates so as to better utilize its resources and diversify its risk.

About three months ago, the Chairman and CEO., Keith Overby set up the M&A committee to research possible acquisition candidates and present its findings at the quarterly board meeting. He asked the committee members to consider firms in related as well as unrelated industries and explain the rationale for their recommendations.

After considerable research, data gathering, and analysis, the committee had narrowed their choices down to three possible candidates. After the presentation at the quarterly meeting in March, the Board of Directors had ruled out two of the three candidates and asked the committee to conduct further valuation and analysis on the third candidate –QuickResolve Products. The board members were particularly curious about the low P/E ratio that the firm was trading at. In fact, one board member had heard about "relative P/E magic" and was wondering whether by acquiring QuickResolve the firm could boost it's P/E ratio and possibly its earnings per share.

QuickResolve Products, headquartered in Rockford, Illinois, was a mid-sized company with assets of $2 billion. The firm's earnings per share had been steadily increasing each year and were currently $1.20 per share. Surprisingly, however, the committee found that although the firm had a fairly well diversified customer base, its P/E ratio was rather low at 12.5X -- much below the average P/E ratio for the industry. The committee felt that one reason for the low P/E ratio might have been the recent retirement of their CEO who had managed the company in a very centralized manner. All managers reported directly to him and he made most of the strategic decisions. His experience and vision had been well rewarded in the market.

The members of the M&A committee felt that if QuickResolve were to be acquired by Innovative Concepts, production and marketing costs could be significantly reduced due to Innovative Concepts' technical and marketing expertise. The incremental net cash flows of the combined company were estimated to be at least $45 million per year for the foreseeable future. Moreover, since QuickResolve was involved in a totally different industrial sector there were some significant diversification benefits to be had.

Tables 1-4 present the financial statements of Innovative Concepts and QuickResolve Products respectively. The finance department of Innovative Concepts' had recently estimated the firm's weighted average cost of capital to be 16% and the required rate of return on equity to be 20%.

Since Dan had first suggested QuickResolve as a possible acquisition candidate, it was his job to provide the Board with the necessary information, clarification, and estimates. Dan firmly believed that QuickResolve and Innovative Concepts were 'made for each other!' Now if only he could convince the board!

Table 1

Innovative Concepts Income Statement ($ millions)	
Revenues	$3,000
Cost of Goods Sold	2,550
Gross Profit	450
Selling & Administration Expenses	100
Depreciation	50
Interest	50
Earnings Before Taxes	250
Taxes (40%)	100
Net Income	150
Dividends Paid ($1 per share on 100 million shares	100
Addition to Retained Earnings	50

Table 2

Innovative Concepts Balance Sheet ($ millions)	
Cash	400
Marketable Securities	200
Accounts Receivable	400
Inventory	1,000
Total Current Assets	2000
Gross Fixed Assets	6000
Accumulated Depreciation	-2000
Net Fixed Assets	4000
Total Assets	6000
Accounts Payables	300
Accruals	200
Notes Payable	500
Total Current Liabilities	1000
Long-term debt	2000
Common Stock (Par Value = $5 per share)	500
Capital Surplus	1000
Retained Earnings	1500
Total Shareholders' Equity	3000
Total Liabilities and Shareholders' Equity	6000

Table 3

QuickResolve Products	
Income Statement ($ millions)	
Revenues	$1,500
Cost of Goods Sold	1,320
Gross Profit	180
Selling & Administration Expenses	50
Depreciation	15
Interest	15
Earnings Before Taxes	100
Taxes (40%)	40
Net Income	60
Dividends Paid ($0.8per share on 50 million shares)	40
Addition to Retained Earnings	20

Table 4

QuickResolve Products Balance Sheet ($ millions)	
Cash	300
Marketable Securities	200
Accounts Receivable	200
Inventory	300
Total Current Assets	1000
Gross Fixed Assets	1400
Accumulated Depreciation	-400
Net Fixed Assets	1000
Total Assets	2000
Accounts Payables	150
Accruals	130
Notes Payable	500
Total Current Liabilities	780
Long-term debt	600
Common Stock (Par Value = $2 per share)	100
Capital Surplus	340
Retained Earnings	180
Total Shareholders' Equity	620
Total Liabilities and Shareholders' Equity	2000

Questions:

1. Using the formula for free cash flow, explain the various reasons why firms undertake mergers and acquisitions? Which of these reasons are most likely to apply to the acquisition that Innovative Concepts is considering?

2. Comment on the director's suggestion of playing the "relative P/E game." For your calculations assume that QuickResolve's shareholders have agreed to an exchange ratio of 1 share of Innovative Concepts for every 2 shares held in QuickResolve. Also, assume that the combined net income of the two firms is the sum of their net incomes prior to the completion of the deal.

3. Using the free cash flow method of valuation calculate the maximum offer price that Innovative Concepts would be justified in making for QuickResolve Products.

4. Let's say that Innovative Concepts is able to close the deal at a price of $1150 $ millions by paying cash or by exchanging 1 of its shares for 2 of QuickResolve's shares. Should it use cash or stock as the payment mechanism? Why? What are the pros and cons of each payment mechanism for the acquiring and the target firm respectively?

5. If QuickResolve wants to block the takeover attempt what can it do? Please explain the rationale and possible outcome of each suggestion.

6.   If the book value of the net fixed assets of QuickResolve are at only 80% of their current market value, and Innovative Concepts decides to step up the basis of the assets for depreciation after the deal is closed, what would the balance sheet of the combined firm look like under the purchase method of accounting for mergers and acquisitions? Assume that the deal is completed at an exchange ratio of 0.5 (i.e. 1 share of Innovative Concepts for 2 shares of QuickResolve)

7.   What are some tax issues that must be considered by Innovative Concepts' management team when making the bid?

8.   One of the M&A committee members had told Dan that the main advantage of this deal to Innovative Concepts is the diversification benefit that exists from the two companies being in totally different industry sectors and that it be stressed the most in the presentation. Do you agree? Explain.

29

Lease Versus Buy Analysis

Why Buy It When You Can Lease It?

Angelo Rossi opened his little "upscale" Italian restaurant almost 25 years ago in the heart of New York City. His specialty was the freshly baked bread oozing with homemade garlic butter and of course, the delicious varieties of pasta and lasagna. The ambience and aroma were simply out of this world and kept bringing the customers back for more.

An immigrant from southern Italy, Angelo put all his savings into his business. With the help of his wife, Maria, and their son Paulo, Angelo kept the restaurant running smoothly and helped it gain tremendous popularity among many New Yorkers. Angelo was always proud of the fact that he owned everything in his restaurant, right from the property on which it stood down to the plates on which the food was served. Everything had been paid for with his own hard-earned cash. Being from the 'old school,' Angelo always believed that to be a debtor is to be a slave to the lender. He, therefore, chose to save up and pay cash for whatever was needed.

Over time the restaurant's clientele grew significantly and the wait times during peak periods became unbearably long. After careful consideration, Angelo relocated the restaurant to a much larger site with ample parking and tables. As always, the move was financed with cash. Then about three years ago, Angelo retired and turned over the business to Paulo. Having watched his dad nurture the business, Paulo, kept up the family tradition of excellent service and personal attention to details.

Along with the business, however, Paulo inherited some worn out equipment, which surely had "seen better days." Paulo was sick and tired of making frequent phone calls to the service company for equipment repairs and maintenance work. As a result, the restaurant service quality was beginning to deteriorate and profits were being hurt. In particular, three ovens, a dishwasher, and a pasta machine needed to be replaced. The total cost of the equipment including delivery and installation was estimated to be $100,000. 3-year Modified Accelerated Cost Recovery schedule rates could be used to depreciate the equipment.

Now if it were Papa Rossi at the helm, there would have been enough cash in the coffer to buy the equipment outright. However, under Paulo, the cash balance of the firm had shrunk miserably. The problem with Paulo was that unlike his father, he enjoyed a much more lavish lifestyle. The flashy sports car, penthouse, and boat were all paid in full from business profits, leaving not much cash for business renovation and equipment replacement. On numerous occasions, Papa Rossi had tried to counsel his son on the benefits of being thrifty but to no avail. Young Paulo preferred to live for today.

Thanks to Papa Rossi's conservative ways the credit rating of the restaurant had been exemplary. The money for the equipment could be easily borrowed from their bank at a rate of 10% per year over a 5-year term. However, Paulo had heard from his business colleagues that in some cases it is better to lease than to buy. Many of his colleagues claimed that they were already enjoying significant benefits as a result of having leased business assets.

After checking around and calling various leasing companies, Paulo found that he could lease the needed equipment and appliances from AAA Leasing Company for an annual lease payment of $25,000 over a 5- year term. The lease would carry an option to buy the equipment for $40,000 at the end of 5 years. Maintenance costs on the new equipment were estimated to be $2,000 per year and would be covered by the annual lease payment. The increased efficiency of the new equipment was expected to result in net cost savings of $4,000 per year.

Paulo, being fully aware of his father's dislike for debt was seriously thinking about leasing the equipment. However, not being fully conversant with all the pros and cons of leasing versus borrowing and buying, there were a number of questions that Paulo needed answers for. Above all, he was curious about AAA Leasing Company's main slogan, which read "Why buy it if you can lease it?"

Questions:

1. What are the different kinds of leases available and which one would be best suited for Paulo's restaurant? Explain why.

2. Calculate the net advantage to leasing (NAL) the restaurant equipment. It is assumed that the old equipment has no resale value whereas the new equipment would have a salvage value of $30,000 after 5 years. The restaurant's tax rate is estimated to be 40%.

3. What do you think typically happens to leased equipment after the term of the lease expires?

4. After doing all the calculations, Paulo realizes that he underestimated the cost savings that would result from improved efficiency by $1000 per year. How should this error be handled? Is it relevant? Explain.

5. How should depreciation and taxes be accounted for in the calculations?

6. If the equipment were to be leased, would the lease payments be tax deductible? Explain.

7. If AAA Leasing Company's tax rate is 40%, what is the minimum lease payment that it would be willing to accept? Explain.

8. What is the maximum lease payment that Paulo should be willing to pay? Explain.

9. How much of an impact does the forecast of the salvage value of the new machine have on the lease versus buy decision?

10. If Paulo leases the equipment, what impact would it have on the firm's debt capacity?

11. Does the size of the business play any role in lease versus buy decisions of this type?

12. Does the type of asset under consideration have much effect on the lease versus buy decision?

13. Are there any other factors that need to be considered in a lease versus borrow and buy decision of this type? Explain.

14. All things considered, should Paulo lease or borrow and buy the equipment? Explain.